# The Somerset & Dorset Files

## No.1

*A Railway Bylines Special*
*By Martin Smith*

4F 0-6-0 44560 – which had been built for the S&D in 1922 – stands at Evercreech Junction on 21 September 1963. *Photograph: P.Gomm; www.transporttreasury.co.uk*

## IRWELL PRESS Ltd.

Copyright IRWELL PRESS LIMITED
ISBN-10 1-903266-87-4
ISBN-13 378-1-903266-87-8
First published in the United Kingdom in 2008
by Irwell Press Limited, 59A, High Street, Clophill,
Bedfordshire MK45 4BE
Printed by Newnorth Print, Bedford
Tel: 01525 861888
Fax: 01525 862044
www.irwellpress.co.uk

*Cover:* S&D 7F 53807 prepares to pull out of Wellow with a northbound goods on 6 July 1959. *Photograph: R.C.Riley; www.transporttreasury.co.uk*

*This page:* An unidentified 8F 2-8-0 strolls across Midford Viaduct with a Down goods on 18 August 1965. *Photograph: Paul Cottrell*

# Acknowledgements

During the preparation of this book, reference was made to S&D, LMS, British Railways and Board of Trade minute books and documents which were sourced at the National Archives, Kew. Reference was also made to *The Somerset & Dorset Railway* by Robin Atthill (David & Charles, 1967), *The History of the Somerset Coalfield* by C.G.Down and A.J.Warrington (David & Charles), *Radstock – Coal and Steam* by Chris Handley (Millstream Books, 1991), *Bailey Gate and the Milk Factory* by Bill Coomer (2000) and to various issues of *Five Arches* (the history journal of the Radstock, Midsomer Norton & District Museum Trust; extracts used in this book have been reproduced with the Society's kind permission), *The Pines Express* (the magazine of the S&D Trust), and various contemporary railway periodicals, especially the *Railway Observer.*

Thanks to the late Bryan L.Wilson and Mr. Eric Youldon for invaluable advice and assistance. Thanks also to Julie Dexter (editor, *Five Arches*) and to the photographers and archivists who made their photographs available for publication. Last but definitely not least, a huge thank you to my ever-patient wife, Micky, who, despite not being able to tell a 7F from a lavatory brush, somehow managed to seem as if she shared my enthusiasm for this project. Bless her.

**Martin Smith, Coleford, Somerset; July 2007**

---

## This one's for Bryan.

---

**Principal dates (opening dates are those when the line opened to public traffic, not the dates of ceremonial openings)**

**28 August 1854:** Highbridge-Glastonbury opened by the Somerset Central Railway

**3 May 1858:** Highbridge-Burnham opened by the Somerset Central Railway

**16 March 1859:** Glastonbury-Wells opened by the Somerset Central Railway

**1 November 1860:** Blandford-Wimborne Jct opened by the Dorset Central Railway

**3 February 1862:** Glastonbury-Cole opened by the Somerset Central Railway

**3 February 1862:** Cole-Templecombe opened by the Dorset Central Railway

**1 September 1862:** Somerset Central and Dorset Central merged to form the Somerset & Dorset Railway

**31 August 1863:** S&D trains permitted to run through to Poole

**10 September 1863:** Templecombe-Blandford opened by the Somerset & Dorset Railway

**15 June 1874:** S&D started running through to Bournemouth West (with aid of running powers over other company's lines)

**20 July 1874:** Evercreech Junction-Bath opened by the S&D

**1 November 1875:** S&D became jointly leased to and administered by the Midland Railway and the London & South Western Railway

**14 December 1885:** Corfe Mullen Jct-Broadstone opened jointly by the MR and the L&SWR

**21 July 1890:** Edington Jct-Bridgwater opened by the Bridgwater Railway (worked by S&DJ from the outset)

**11 July 1920:** Corfe Mullen Jct-Wimborne Jct closed to passenger traffic

**1 January 1930:** S&D locos taken into LMS stock; rolling stock and infrastructure became the responsibility of Southern Railway

**1 January 1948:** Nationalisation; on 2 February the S&D system was assigned to the Southern Region of British Railways

**2 April 1950:** The S&D north of Cole transferred to Western Region administration for commercial and administrative matters but the operating of the whole line remained with the Southern Region

**29 October 1951:** Highbridge-Burnham closed to ordinary passenger traffic (occasionally used by excursion trains and other specials until 8 September 1962; goods continued until 20 May 1963)

**29 October 1951:** Glastonbury-Wells closed to all traffic

**1 December 1952:** Edington Junction-Bridgwater closed to passenger traffic (goods continued until 1 October 1954)

**17 September 1956:** Stourpaine & Durweston, Charlton Marshall, Spetisbury and Corfe Mullen halts closed

**1 February 1958:** Western Region took over responsibility for operations on the Bath-Templecombe section (the WR boundary now extending to a point between Templecombe and Henstridge); locos at Bath, Radstock, Templecombe and Highbridge sheds transferred to WR stock

**2 August 1965:** Bournemouth West 'temporarily' closed to S&D trains due to engineering work; some S&D trains diverted to Bournemouth Central, others started and terminated at Branksome. (S&D trains did not return to Bournemouth West; the station officially closed on 4 October.)

**7 March 1966:** Most of S&D system closed completely; Green Park station also closed. Four sections remained open to goods traffic – their closure dates were:

**30 November 1967:** Bath Junction-Bath Co-op Siding (Twerton) – had been used for coal traffic for the Co-op

**6 January 1969:** Blandford-Broadstone – had been used for goods and milk

**3 October 1972:** Bason Bridge-Highbridge – had been used for milk traffic from Bason Bridge and latterly fly ash to Highbridge

**19 November 1973:** Writhlington Colliery-Radstock – since 1966, coal traffic had been taken out via a new connection to the GWR's Bristol-Frome branch at Radstock

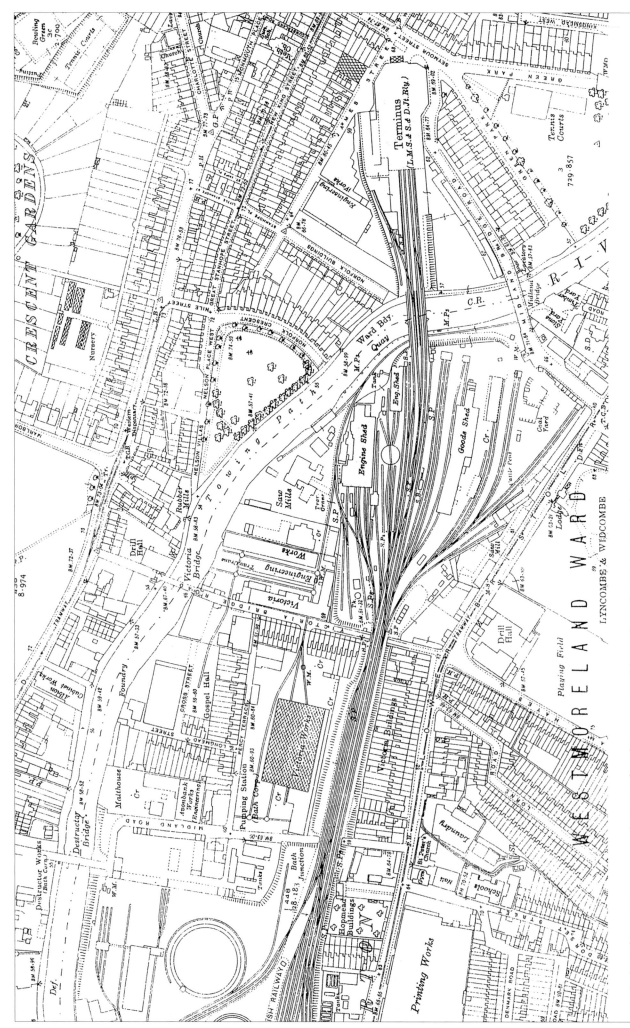

25-inch Ordnance Survey map of 1930 reduced to approx 17½in to the mile. *Crown Copyright*

4

# Bath

The Somerset & Dorset line between Bath and Bournemouth positively brimmed with character. It was wonderfully individualistic in so many ways – so much so that, if one were to ask a dozen railway enthusiasts what each one of them particularly liked about the S&D, one would get a dozen different answers. So to kick off this photographic tribute to the S&D we have a picture which shows just a few aspects of the line's special appeal: we have the 'Pines Express', we have double-heading and we have the approach to Bath – one of the most famous and historic cities in the country. The picture is believed to have been taken in 1955. The northbound 'Pines Express' approaches Green Park station, with 2P 40563 piloting Standard Class 5 4-6-0 73052. If the train was on time the picture will have been taken a few minutes before midday, the northbound 'Pines' being due at Green Park at 11.50am on Mondays-Fridays or at 12.01pm on Saturdays. The lead engine is crossing the bridge over Victoria Bridge Road; the line diverging to the right on the near side of the bridge leads to the engine sheds. The picture was, in fact, taken from the top of the water softening plant reaction tank in the shed yard. The backs of the houses on the far side of the line are those of Victoria Buildings which front on to the Lower Bristol Road. The old house in Victoria Bridge Road itself has gone, as have all the other buildings in the road. In the distance just behind the last coach of the train is Bath Junction; the old Midland line to Bristol continues to the right of the signal box while the S&D line diverges to the left of the 'box. *Photograph: D.T.Flook*

5

*Left.* Express traffic – it says so on the hood. This picture was taken outside Green Park station on 5 September 1950; even though the major railway companies had started to use battery-electric vehicles in the early 1900s and internal-combustion vehicles from around the time of World War I, by 1950 there were still many horse-drawn vehicles in use for town and city deliveries. The 'LMS' lettering on the vehicle here is not at all remarkable; although British Railways came into existence on 1 January 1948, countless items of railway equipment and machinery retained evidence of their pre-Nationalisation ownership for many years afterwards.
*Photograph: M.N.Bland; www.transporttreasury.co.uk*

*Bottom right.* Standard Class 5 4-6-0 73012 crosses the River Avon on the approach to Bath Green Park with the 12 noon from Templecombe on 4 April 1963. The date on which 73012 had come to the S&D is a bit of a mystery as its transfer to Green Park shed at Bath seems to have gone unrecorded. *Photograph: David Idle; www.transporttreasury.co.uk*

Another aspect of the S&D's appeal was that because of its heritage as a 'Joint' line – for more than seventy years it had been jointly owned and worked by the Midland Railway and the London & South Western Railway and their respective successors – even in British Railways days one saw engines, trains and infrastructure that seemed out of place. To illustrate that point we have a picture of a former Southern Railway engine at what was originally a Midland Railway station amid what was, in geographical terms, predominantly Great Western territory. The engine is Bulleid Pacific 34041 *Wilton*. It is standing at Platform 2 at Green Park station with the 7.05pm stopper to Bournemouth West – the last through S&D train of the day – on 29 May 1963. The train was timed to take 3 hours 17 minutes for the 71½-mile journey. Although the station is invariably remembered as Green Park, for much of its life it was listed in *Bradshaws'* as Queen Square. The Green Park suffix was not brought into 'official' use until June 1951. The station pre-dated the S&D. It had been opened by the Midland Railway as the terminus of its branch from Bristol to Bath (via Kelston and Weston) on 4 August 1869. That said, the station was only partly finished at that time – it was not fully completed until 7 May 1870. The Midland granted running powers over the Bath end of the line to the S&D, so when the S&D opened its famous extension from Evercreech Junction to Bath on 20 July 1874 its trains had full use of the station. The *Tourists' Descriptive Guide to the Somerset & Dorset Railway*, which was printed and published by James Keene in 1874, described Bath station in the rather gushing manner which was typical of the period: 'In front of the station, which is of handsome design, fluted pillars with carved capitols support a neat balustrade. There is plenty of room in front of the station which is close to the fashionable neighbourhood of Green-park. The centre of the city, in which the Market-place, Abbey and Guildhall stand, is only five minutes walk from the station, and in passing up Kingsmead-street many houses, which were formerly tenanted by noblemen and the higher classes, the street hereabouts having comprised "Old Bath", will be seen. On entering the station the visitor is at once struck by its extreme lightness, good ventilation and beauty of design. The plants and rock-work which hide the buffers are a pleasing novelty. The sidings within the station are spanned by a broad iron girder roof covered with plate glass nearly a quarter of an inch in thickness. On either side there are spacious platforms covered to the extent of 100 yards, and uncovered they extend a similar distance. Charming views are obtained from these platforms into the fields which slope up the hills in the neighbourhood, the same being diversified by numerous elegant villas; the stores of the 2nd Somerset Militia are in the immediate foreground, and on the right the commencement of the rapidly growing village of Twerton. Messrs. Spiers & Ponds have extremely convenient refreshment-rooms on the platform, which is also well supplied with waiting-rooms, and in fact every other accommodation, whilst closely adjacent is the city of Bath, every portion of which is pregnant with interest'. Phew! *Photograph: Hugh Ballantyne*

*Left.* 9F 2-10-0 92220 *Evening Star* waits at Green Park station with the 1.10pm to Templecombe on 4 September 1963. The 9Fs had come to the Somerset & Dorset in 1960 principally to look after the heaviest through trains. They did very well but, ironically, they lost some of their principal duties after only a couple of years as, from September 1962, the heavy, long-distance through trains – the very trains for which the locos were intended – were diverted away from the S&D. So the line's 9Fs filled in with less-demanding jobs such as the three-coach Bath-Templecombe stopper in this picture. *Photograph: Hugh Ballantyne*

*Bottom left.* The LMS-built 2P 4-4-0s of 1928-32 were a development of a Midland design, and a number of them were based on the S&D where they proved to be useful and versatile machines. Indeed, three were actually built specially for the S&D. One of those three eventually became BR 40634 – that loco is seen here piloting Standard Class 5 4-6-0 73047 on the ferocious 1 in 50 climb from Bath Junction towards Devonshire Tunnel and on to Combe Down tunnel on a beautifully crisp 4 February 1961. As an aid to getting one's bearings, the overbridge just around the bend took the appropriately named Bridge Road across the railway at Twerton. This part of the trackbed is now a linear park. *Photograph: Peter Barnfield*

*Below.* 2P 4-4-0 40569 and 9F 2-10-0 92001 have emerged from the south end of Combe Down Tunnel with the southbound 'Pines Express' and are crossing the 95 yard-long Tucking Mill Viaduct over Horsecombe Vale. Although invariably known as Tucking Mill viaduct, on 'official' S&D maps and plans the structure was titled Combe Vale Viaduct. When the Midford-Radstock section of the line was doubled in 1892-94 the intention was to extend the double-track section northwards from Midford to the south end of Combe Down Tunnel, and Tucking Mill Viaduct was rebuilt to double-track width. Space was also prepared near the viaduct for a station to serve Combe Down. But as the history books – and this picture – show, the Combe Down-Midford section was never doubled, nor did Combe Down get a station of its own. Tucking Mill Viaduct still stands today, but barriers are in place at either end so there is no public access. But there is better news concerning the section of the old trackbed between the south end of the viaduct and Midford – that section, although privately owned, now has public footpath status. *Photograph: George Heiron; www.transporttreasury.co.uk*

# Midford

By far the best-known train on the S&D was the 'Pines Express'. This picture shows the southbound 'Pines' crossing Midford Viaduct, a few yards south of the station, on 26 August 1961. The train was scheduled to leave Manchester (Piccadilly) at 10.00am; on Mondays-Fridays the scheduled arrival at Bournemouth West was 5.32pm or 6.08pm on Saturdays. The return working left Bournemouth at 9.45am. After the cessation of the long-distance through trains on the S&D in September 1962 the 'Pines' was re-routed via Southampton and Oxford. In this picture the train is headed by 2P 4-4-0 40564 and the rebuilt Bulleid Pacific 34046 *Braunton*. The latter loco was saved for preservation and at the time of writing is undergoing extensive restoration at the West Somerset Railway at Minehead. Sadly, not one of the Midland- or LMS-built 2P 4-4-0s was saved; given the versatility of these locos – not to mention their good looks – this must be regarded as an opportunity lost. Getting back to the matter of the S&D line at Midford… Note that the line has become double track part way across the viaduct. When the line was built it was single, but as mentioned in one of the earlier photo captions the Midford-Radstock section was doubled in 1892-94; with the line between Radstock and Templecombe having been doubled in a piecemeal manner between 1884 and 1892, there was now double track all the way from Midford to Templecombe. *Photograph: Hugh Ballantyne*

*Left.* The fireman of Saltley shed's 'Black Five' 44965 prepares to exchange the single-line tablet as it drifts into the beautiful little station at Midford on 11 July 1960. The station was situated adjacent to the Hope & Anchor pub and, these days, the part of the old trackbed between the north end of the Midford Viaduct and the south end of the platform has been incorporated into the pub car park. The name of the Hope & Anchor, incidentally, harks back to the days of the Somersetshire Coal Canal which used to pass through Midford. The canal had opened in 1805 and, in its entirety, extended from Dundas Basin on the Kennet & Avon Canal to Paulton, with a branch to Radstock, but like most of the nation's canals it lost much of its traffic to the railways in the latter half of the 1800s. It closed in 1898. *Photograph: R.C.Riley; www.transporttreasury.co.uk*

*Below.* A 2P 4-4-0 pilots a Standard Class 5 4-6-0 on the northbound 'Pines Express' through Midford on 10 March 1955. The herbaceous single-track line crossing from right to left in the foreground is – or rather was – the old GWR branch from Limpley Stoke to Hallatrow, which passed under Midford Viaduct. The GWR branch had lost its passenger services as long ago as 1925 but the Limpley Stoke-Camerton section had remained open to goods traffic – principally coal from Camerton Colliery – until February 1951. But that was not the very end for the branch as it had a famous – a *very* famous – resuscitation in July/August 1952 when it was used for the filming of *The Titfield Thunderbolt*. Those who have seen the film (and that must surely be everyone who is reading this book!) will be familiar with the opening sequence showing the 'Titfield' engine – a Great Western 14XX class 0-4-2T – passing under Midford Viaduct while an S&D train crosses the viaduct. This, of course, required the passages of the 14XX and the S&D train to be coordinated so that each was in the right spot at the right time, but although the film crew had control over 'their' 14XX, they had no control whatsoever over the trains on the S&D line. The S&D trains were ordinary service workings – i.e. not laid on specially for the filming – and so the film crew had to time the 'run up' of the 14XX to perfection so that it passed under the viaduct at precisely the right moment. Despite several preliminary test runs to work out the timing the film crew didn't get it quite right when the cameras were actually rolling, with the result that the two trains were not in the frame simultaneously. Nor did it work the second time; nor the third.... It took eight takes before that famous opening sequence was in the can! *Photograph: Hugh Ballantyne*

# Radstock

RADSTOCK
REPAIR AND PAINTING OF STATION

    With reference to minute No.696 of the Joint Conference, it was reported that at the request of the Engineer tenders had been obtained for the execution of necessary works of repair and painting at Radstock Station and Writhlington Signal Box, including the painting of the signals and point rods, and that, with the approval of the Managements, the offer of Messrs. C. and T. Painters, Ltd., to carry out the works for the inclusive price of £362 had been accepted.

               Approved.

**Left.** Bulleid Pacific 34099 *Lynmouth* passes Waterloo Cottages on the approach to Radstock with a southbound train on 22 July 1958. The train has just passed under the bridge carrying the tramway from the old Tyning Colliery. The spoil tips can be seen poking above the houses on the left. The wooded hill immediately beyond the rear of the train is another spoil tip; the effort of planting it with trees – a comparatively early exercise in landscaping – had clearly been worthwhile. Tyning Colliery had ceased working in 1909 and had been abandoned in 1922 but the tramway had remained in use for tipping spoil from Ludlows Colliery and Middle Pit until 1954. This picture provides the first glimpse of the principal *raison d'être* of the S&D's 'Bath Extension' – namely coal. Radstock was the centre of the north Somerset coalfield; over a period of around 200 years there have been nineteen pits within a mile or so of the centre of Radstock, albeit not all operational simultaneously. The Great Western Railway had opened a mineral railway between Radstock and Frome as early as 1854, but when the GWR proclaimed its support for a new line between Radstock and Bristol in the late 1860s the S&D feared that it might lose out completely on the potentially lucrative coal traffic. The S&D's answer was the 'Bath Extension' – the famous 26-mile long line between Evercreech Junction and Bath, via Radstock. Work on the line was completed in just two years – a remarkable feat, especially in view of the nature of terrain it had to cross – and it opened on 20 July 1874. The GWR-backed Radstock-Bristol line had opened the previous year and had started to secure some of Radstock's coal traffic, but the S&D also secured its own share of the coal traffic, six of the pits in the town being connected to or served by the S&D. At its peak in the early 1900s the North Somerset Coalfield as a whole yielded 1,250,000 tons of coal per annum. By 1920 there were still 26 pits at work, employing around 10,000 men and boys and producing 1,167,800 tons. Although production gradually dropped – Somerset coal was excellent quality but the seams were narrow and difficult to work and, moreover, by the 1940s the pits were the least mechanised in the country – by the time the coal industry was nationalised in 1947 there were still four working pits at Radstock and, between them, they were producing around 200,000 tons annually. Two of those four pits – Braysdown and Lower Writhlington – were still served by the S&D. The last of the Radstock collieries to remain in production was Lower Writhlington which, in its later years, was connected underground to Kilmersdon Colliery. When winding ceased in September 1973 it brought an end to the mining industry in North Somerset. The North Somerset Coalfield thereby claimed the dubious distinction of being the first coalfield in the country to cease working completely. *Photograph: R.C.Riley; www.transporttreasury.co.uk*

**Bottom left.** In the previous picture caption we mentioned the tramway from Tyning Colliery. The tramway crossed the S&D's main running lines on a bridge of standard height, but the bridge which took it over the nearby goods sidings had only 10ft 5in headroom. This picture of said bridge was taken on 22 July 1958. The bridge was known locally as 'Marble Arch'; its restricted clearance meant that only suitably 'low height' locomotives could pass underneath. As noted elsewhere, although Tyning Colliery had been abandoned in 1922 (it had ceased to draw coal in 1909 but had continued to pump water until 1922) the tramway had remained in use for tipping spoil from Ludlows Pit. Somewhat ironically, almost all of the rail-borne output from Ludlows went via the GWR, not the S&D, so it was the spoil tramway of a GWR customer which dictated the height of the shunting locomotives used by the S&D. *Photograph: R.C.Riley; www.transporttreasury.co.uk*

**Inset.** S&D Joint Committee minutes, 4 November 1936

Radstock town centre as it was in the 1960s.

*Top.* It is October 1956, and the photographer is standing on top of 'Marble Arch' to take this picture which looks towards Radstock. The running lines to Bath exit right. The station is just out of view beyond the footbridge in the distance on the right. The tall building to the left of the footbridge is the old Co-op bakery; built in 1909 to replace an earlier bakery, it was provided with its own railway siding in 1914. The bakery closed in the 1950s but the building still stands, its lower storey now being used as a furniture showroom. On the left is the engine shed; alongside the shed a 'Jinty' is blowing off (if you'll pardon the expression). The track curving away to the left in the foreground goes to Ludlows Colliery (which ceased winding in 1954) and continues through the colliery yard to join up with the GWR's Bristol-Radstock Frome branch. Although that line gave a physical connection between the S&D and the GWR, as far as can be determined it was never used for the exchange of traffic between the two railways. As noted in the previous photo caption, most of the output of Ludlows Colliery went via the GWR. The little that went via the S&D was dispatched in wagons which were hauled by horses – a 'team of great black shire horses with white fetlocks' – across the Frome Road to sidings alongside the S&D. Even though Ludlows provided the S&D with only a little coal traffic, it *did* provide some of the coal for the S&D engine shed at Radstock. This coal came directly from the colliery in small tubs; at the shed the tubs were winched up on a gantry and tipped into the locos' bunkers or tenders. As a final word (for now, at least) about the connecting line between the S&D and GWR via Ludlows Colliery, it also provided a means of getting wagons across to Marcrofts Wagon Works which were alongside the GWR's Frome branch line ¼-mile south of the GWR station. *Photograph: Derek Clayton*

*Bottom.* This superb picture shows BR Class 4 4-6-0 75007 crossing the road on the approach to Radstock North station with the 11.40am Bournemouth West-Bristol on Thursday 5 September 1963. The station had obtained its 'North' suffix as recently as 26 September 1949; on that same date the nearby ex-GWR station had been suffixed Radstock West. Hitherto, both had been named Radstock, but as all the locals knew which station was which, and as the two establishments had been under different ownership (one 'Joint Committee', one GWR) prior to 1948, there had been little confusion. With the level crossing closed across the road, cars wait at the bottom of Bath New Road. The ex-GWR Bristol-Radstock-Frome branch crossed the same road only a few yards to the left and the presence of two level crossings in such close proximity caused problems for road users. There were problems even in the days of horse-drawn traffic; as long ago as 1875 the Board of Trade had ordered the S&D and the GWR to replace the level crossings with road bridges but, as the history books show, the S&D and the GWR successfully ignored the order. Inevitably, the problem of the two adjacent crossings became more acute as time passed, especially in the motor car era. For example, it was reported on August Bank Holiday Monday 1937 – a fine day when car-owners were out in force and the railway trains to and from the seaside were well-patronised – that 'upwards of forty cars at a time' were forced to wait at one or other of the crossings. Somewhat ironically, earlier that very month the Minister of Transport, Leslie Burgin (who had replaced Leslie Hore-Belisha in May of that year), had announced his wish to abolish all level crossings on major highways within seven years; but that was no good to those who were queuing at Radstock on the Bank Holiday and, of course, it did not happen anyway. After the war the nation's holiday habits gradually returned to normal – for the majority, that meant travelling by train – and by the early 1950s the S&D was once again very well used. On summer Saturdays at that time there were around 85 train or engine movements (including 24 reliefs) over the S&D level crossing at Radstock and a further 20 on the GWR (though the latter line was not so heavily influenced by summer Saturday holiday traffic). Many of these train movements were concentrated into certain times; for example, 22 trains crossed one or other of the roads between 11am and 1pm – an average of one every five minutes. Motorists often became very irate and it was far from uncommon for the signalmen to be threatened, so during peak hours a policeman was usually stationed by the gates to keep the peace. In the background of this picture we have the Waldegrave Arms and, on the right, is the much-windowed Market Hall. The Market Hall was at one time owned by the Coombs family who were, perhaps, best-known to earlier generations of Radstock folk for their beer. The family originally came from the small village of Camerton, a couple of miles to the north of Radstock; they were innkeepers but, as was the usual practice in 18th and 19th centuries, they brewed their own beer. In the 1850s George Coombs left Clandown and acquired the Bell Inn at Radstock; he was later joined by his cousin, Joseph. The pair also acquired the Lamb Inn at Clandown and, later, the Waldegrave Inn at Radstock, brewing being undertaken at all three of their premises. Their main brew was Clandown Bitter, which became widely sold in the West Country. They established Coombs' Clandown and Radstock Breweries and Hotels Company Limited, and by the late 1800s the company owned numerous inns, several hotels (including the Bell Hotel at Radstock, built in 1880 to replace the former Bell Inn), houses and land in and around the Radstock area and, by way of bringing us back to square one, in 1898 they erected Radstock Market Hall, the building in which Radstock Museum is now situated. As for the members of the Coombs family, the 1881 census shows that George Coombs was living at Radstock House (now the premises of Radstock Workingmen's Club) with his wife (who, incidentally, is listed in the census at being born at Farleigh Castle – to the best of our knowledge this was an alternative name for the village of Farleigh Hungerford, the actual castle having been in ruins since the late 1600s), a housekeeper and a servant. Turning now to Joseph Coombs, for many years he lived 'above the shop' at the Bell Hotel from where he conducted his business, but by 1901 he was living at The Firs on the new Bath Road at Radstock. Coombs' Brewery carried on until 1922 when it was sold to the Oakhill Brewery Company. Some of the older equipment was resold to Fussell & Sons' Cross Keys Brewery in the village of Rode, near the Somerset/Wiltshire border. *Photograph: David Idle; www.transporttreasury.co.uk*

# Midsomer Norton

A fascinating study of station ephemera at the north end of the Down platform at Midsomer Norton in June 1964. *Photograph: Peter Barnfield*

*Left.* 9F 2-10-0 92233 approaches Midsomer Norton with a northbound express on 11 August 1962. (Ignore the '1094' board above the buffer beam – this referred to the Down working that had taken the engine south and, clearly, had not been removed.) This being a summer Saturday, the chances are that the train is a long-distance through working for the Midlands or the North, in which case it will not be stopping at Midsomer Norton. Some of the northbound through trains ran non-stop over the S&D and, for those that did stop, the last call was Evercreech or Shepton Mallet. As for the 9Fs, the class were first seen at Bath in 1956 – the first visit is thought to be that of 92049 of Toton shed on 31 July of that year – but until 1960 they worked only northwards. As far as can be determined the first appearance of a 9F on the S&D itself was on 29 March 1960 when 92204 of St.Philips Marsh shed in Bristol hauled a test train from Bath to Bournemouth West and back. The purpose of the test was to see if the 9Fs, despite having been designed for heavy freight work, would be suitable for passenger work over the Mendip Hills; the S&D had, after all, had an almost eternal quest for suitably muscular motive power for the heavy summer passenger trains on the ferociously graded line. With a load of eleven coaches (350 tons), 92204 performed very well; according to a local report it 'started up the 1 in 80 from Blandford like an engine and brake'. The trials having been deemed successful, four of the class, 92203-92206, were transferred to Green Park shed for the summer; for duties on the S&D they were necessarily fitted with Whitaker tablet apparatus. Their presence considerably helped the motive power situation on the line during the summer; they worked the heaviest through trains – including the 'Pines Express' in both directions – and also the 9.03am Bristol-Bournemouth and the 3.40pm Bournemouth-Bath. As just one example of how well they did, a visitor to the line enthusiastically reported that, when travelling behind a 9F on the 2.50pm Bath-Bournemouth (ex-Bradford) on 26 August 1961, the train left Bath 53 minutes late but was ½ minute early at Bournemouth. Not bad! Various other members of the class were drafted to the line for the summers of 1961, 1962, 1963 and 1964. They usually departed at the end of each summer period, their lack of steam heating rendering them unsuitable for passenger work during the winter. As noted in one of the earlier photo captions, although the 9Fs had been intended for the heaviest trains on the line, the long-distance through trains ceased in September 1962 so in subsequent summers they often filled in with lightweight local stopping trains. It was hardly what they had been designed for. *Photograph: R.C.Riley; www.transporttreasury.co.uk*

Photographed from the north end of the Up platform at Midsomer Norton, 'Jinty' 47557 prepares to shunt a rake of empty wagons from the Up line, across to the Down line, and then back into Norton Hill Colliery. The date is 17 September 1963. The line to the colliery can be seen to the right of the S&D running lines; we will be seeing more of the colliery itself in one of the other books in this series. *Photograph: P.Gomm; www.transporttreasury.co.uk*

# The Somerset & Dorset 7F 2-8-0s

At various points in this series of books we meet up with the S&D's famous 7F 2-8-0s. So a closer look at these engines is in order…

*'The first of the new "Consolidation" mineral locomotives for the Somerset and Dorset Joint Railway, which had been built at Derby to the designs of Mr.H.Fowler, chief mechanical engineer of the Midland Railway, arrived at Bath on Sunday, March 1st. We hear that another five of these engines are to be built, and it is anticipated that they will do a lot towards relieving the congested traffic of the Somerset & Dorset line. The new engines will deal with loads 50 per cent heavier than those previously hauled over the steep grades of the line, but "banking" will still be resorted to over the sections where this practice has hitherto been observed.*

*No. 80 is painted black, with the number painted on the sides of the cab instead of being shown in raised brass figures. At present there is no turntable on the Somerset & Dorset line where these engines can be turned, hence the provision of the double cab for protection when running tender first. The tablet changing apparatus used in single line working is fitted on both sides of the tender for the same reason'.* That was how the first of the S&D's famous 7F 2-8-0s was introduced to the public in the 15 April 1914 edition of *The Locomotive* magazine.

The S&D had needed more-powerful locomotives for some time; hitherto its largest goods engines had been 0-6-0s which were basically adaptations of standard Midland Railway designs. In 1906/07 the Midland (which, since the 'Joint' agreement of 1875, had had ultimate responsibility for motive power matters on the S&D) had offered the S&D a choice of two designs of purpose-built 0-8-0s, but the offer had been rejected as, in order to run such engines, almost £35,000 would have had to be spent on bridge strengthening, relaying of track and the lengthening of sidings to accommodate longer trains. In 1911 the S&D had reconsidered the case for the 0-8-0s. This time, it had been suggested that, if a 6-ton reduction in axleweights could be achieved by the use of a leading bogie or pony truck, an eight-coupled engine could be catered for. The result was the 2-8-0s. The first (S&D No.80) was delivered in February 1914; two more (Nos.81 and 82) followed in March, another two (83 and 84) in April and a sixth (85) in August. The cost was £3,500 per engine.

### The new engines
The design of the 2-8-0s is usually routinely credited to Henry Fowler who was, at the time, the Midland Railway's Chief Mechanical Engineer, but the design should correctly be attributed to the drawing office staff at Derby, particularly James Clayton who later joined the SE&CR and worked under Richard Maunsell at Ashford.

The 2-8-0s displayed certain radical departures from standard Derby practices. Not only were they the first eight-coupled engines to be built there, but they were also Derby's first two-cylinder mineral engines to have *outside* cylinders and Walschaert's valve gear.

The engines' nominal tractive effort of 35,932lb was higher than that of any other Midland locomotives, and was only surpassed in 1919 when 'Big Bertha', the 0-10-0 Lickey Banker, was built. The boilers used for the 2-8-0s were, however, standard Derby items, the same type as used for the Deeley compound 4-4-0s. They were the S&D's first superheated engines. The general soundness of the 2-8-0s' design was such that it was used as the basis for the original designs for ROD engines for World War I. Indeed, had it not been for the S&D engines' width over the cylinders, they would probably have become *the* standard ROD design.

On their native territory the 2-8-0s quickly proved to be well-suited to the notoriously difficult Bath-Evercreech section S&D line. However, there seems to have been a degree of corporate foot-shooting as a pair of bridges on the entrance roads to the engine shed at Bath were not strong enough to accept the engines. Until the bridges were rebuilt in 1915 the 2-8-0s had to be shedded at Radstock. But this alternative was not without its problems as, due to the limited clearance under the roof of Radstock shed, the locomotives had to be shorn of their cab roof vents and the upper sections of their chimneys. Another problem – albeit one which had been recognised (see the earlier extract from *The Locomotive* magazine) – was that the engines were too long to be turned on the 46ft 'table at Bath shed. Instead, the practice was for the engines to run chimney-first on southbound trips and tender-first in the northbound direction. This practice prevailed until

1935 when a new 60ft turntable was installed at Bath. Turning at Templecombe was no problem as there had been a 50ft 'table there since the 1880s; turning at the southern end of the line could be undertaken on the triangle at Branksome, although it was not the original intention that the 2-8-0s should work through to Branksome regularly.

Another problem arose when the engines had to go to Highbridge Works for repairs. Because of the weight limitations on the Evercreech-Highbridge section, most of the locomotives' non-essential fitments had to be removed. This ceased to be a problem in 1930 when Highbridge works closed, all major repairs subsequently being undertaken at Derby.

## More of the same

By the mid-1920s the S&D was in desperate need of additional heavy freight engines, so five more 2-8-0s were ordered. Rather than build the engines 'in house' at Derby, the order was placed with Robert Stephenson & Co of Darlington. The price was £6,570 per engine.

The five new engines (S&D Nos.86-90) were delivered in July and August 1925. They displayed significant differences to their predecessors, the main one being the use of a non-standard boiler which was almost six inches larger in diameter than the boilers of the six original engines. Another differential was they were paired with smaller Fowler tenders which held only 5½ tons of coal and were considerably

shorter than the 7-ton tenders of the earlier engines. The earlier engines eventually had their 7-ton tenders replaced by 5½-ton tenders but the last swap did not take place until 1960.

Of the new engines, No.86 participated in the Stockton & Darlington (the *other* S&D!) centenary celebrations at Shildon in 1925, though it did not actually arrive until after the main event – the parade of 2 July. Although the 2-8-0s were intended primarily for mineral workings between Bath and Evercreech Junction, in 1926 several of them were noted on passenger workings to and from Bournemouth; this was a knock-on effect of the General Strike which had brought about a huge reduction in the engines' customary duties – i.e. the movement of coal. It seems that the 2-8-0s performed satisfactorily on passenger duties as, although the coal traffic resumed, in the summer of 1927 it was far from uncommon to see the engines working into Bournemouth with excursion trains from the LMS.

Another of the 2-8-0s, No.88, ventured much farther afield in 1926/27 when it underwent dynamometer car tests for the LMS, being tried against ex-LNWR 0-8-0s on the Toton-Brent coal trains in 1926/27. The 0-8-0s were found to be more thermally efficient than the 2-8-0s and, despite the formers' penchant for overheated axleboxes, as a result of the trials the LMS subsequently opted for a new but rather outdated type of 0-8-0 – the G3s.

## LMS days

The S&D underwent a major

**53806 gallops up the 1 in 50 Devonshire Bank at Bath with the 2.00pm goods to Evercreech Junction on 6 August 1963. Magnificent! This picture shows that there is a tablet catcher on the 'off side' of the tender; unlike the S&D's passenger engines the 7Fs were frequently used tender-first, so they were necessarily fitted with tablet catchers on both sides of their tenders. Photograph: Hugh Ballantyne**

administrative upheaval on 1 January 1930. One aspect was that all S&D locomotives were taken into LMS stock. The 2-8-0s were renumbered 9670-9680 but, when the LMS ordered new G3 0-8-0s in 1932, the 9670 sequence had to be vacated for them so the 2-8-0s were renumbered again, this time 13800-13810. Under LMS auspices the 2-8-0s were famously classified 7F. During the Stanier regime at Derby the 7Fs had new tyres fitted to the driving wheels. The tyres increased the wheel diameter to 4ft 8½in and thereby reduced the locomotives' nominal tractive effort to 35,620lb.

As for the engines' duties during LMS days, they spent most of their time doing what they had been designed for – freight working on the northern section of the S&D line. There were few recorded instances of them wandering far from home, but among the few instances are the temporary departures of 9671, 9676 and 9680 (as they then were) to the Midlands in 1931 for use on heavy Toton-Brent coal trains. The 7Fs were sighted at Gloucester at various times but those instances were usually explained by the engines requiring a

## ENGINE RECORD CARD

E.R.O. 19002

*Southern* ~~A.~~ Region or ~~Division.~~ Name _____  Number **53800**

Class (M.P.) **7F**  Type _____  Built by **DERBY**  Date **FEB/1914**

~~PASSENGER~~ ~~TENDER~~ SUPERHEATER  Wheel arrgt. **2-8-0**  Wheel base (E. & T.) **50 · 1** ft. ins.

FREIGHT ~~TANK NON-SUPERHEATER *~~  Diameter of driving wheels **4 · 8½** ft. ins.

Engine & Tender—Weight in working order **E 64. 15.** T. C. / **T. 45. 2.**  Overall height from rail level **13 · 4** ft. ins.

No. of cylinders **2**  Dia. **21** ins. Stroke **28** ins.  Overall length over buffers (E. & T.) **59 · 9¾** ft. ins.

Class of boiler **G9AS.**

Heating Surface **2907·5 1314.0** sq. ft. **290.7**  No. of tubes { **21 / 146** Large **STEEL** Dia. **5¼** ins. / **188** Small Dia. **1¾** ins.

Boiler pressure **190** lbs. per sq. inch  Firebox grate area **28·4** sq. feet

Tractive effort at 85% B.P. **35296** lbs.  Type of motion **WALSCHAERT**

Radius of minimum curve **6** chains (or **4½** chains dead slow)  Feed pump † **R.** H. Drive

Brakes † **Stm. Eng. Vac. Train.**  Valves † **PISTON.**  Tablet Catching Apparatus † **WHITTAKER.**

Injectors (Type & Size) **LS FLOOD No10 RH HOT WATER No10 LH.**  Mechanical Lubrication* { Cylinders / Axle boxes  ~~Atomiser Lubrication~~ / ~~Fountain Lubrication~~

Axle boxes (Coupled wheels) † ____ **W.1**

CARRIAGE WARMING APPARATI ;* { ~~Front-end~~ ~~Tender-end~~ ~~Both-ends~~ Without  SANDING { Steam ✓ ~~Mechanical~~ Back ~~De-sanding~~  WATER PICK-UP APPARATUS * { ~~Forward direction~~ ~~Both directions~~ ~~Internal fittings only~~ Without

SPECIAL FITTINGS:—

~~Rocking grate~~ ~~Hopper ashpan~~ ~~Self-cleaning Smokebox~~ ~~Smokebox deflector plates~~ ~~Spark arrester~~ ~~V.C.R.~~

Revg. Gear { Screw ~~Lever~~ ~~Power~~  ~~Speed Indicator~~ ~~Roller Bearings~~ ~~Vacuum pump~~ Continuous blowdown ~~Blow-off cock~~ ~~A.T.C.~~

~~Drip cocks~~ ~~Condenser~~ ~~Sand gun~~ ~~Gangway doors~~ ~~Storm Sheets~~ ~~Back Cab~~ ~~Limousine Cab~~

~~Tender weather boards~~ ~~Coal bunker access doors~~ ~~Coal rails~~ ~~Coal pusher~~ ~~Fitted for Snow plough~~

Coal bunker access doors.

*—Delete items not applicable.  †—State type.  [P.T.O.

---

wheel drop, which was something Bath shed did not possess.

Although the 7Fs had occasionally been used to help out with summer Saturday passenger workings to Bournemouth in the 1920s, the engines were rarely used for that purpose in the 1930s. This was partly because the LMS had drafted a number of additional 4-4-0s to the S&D. The need to use the 7Fs on passenger duties was even further reduced in 1938 when LMS 'Black Five' 4-6-0s were introduced on the S&D. The 7Fs were a little more prone to wandering during World War II. They were not infrequently seen at Gloucester and Birmingham; it is likely that at least some of these trips would have been when the engines were 'working their passage', so to speak, to and from

works visits at Derby, but a frustratingly brief comment in the January 1943 edition of the *Railway Observer* noted that '...there is nearly always one and often two of the 7Fs on Saltley shed on a Sunday'. Clearly, such frequent sightings at Saltley would not all have been accounted for by trips to and from Derby Works.

In the opposite direction, in early 1945 several of the 7Fs were observed south of Blandford, though details of their duties were not recorded.

**British Railways**

Following Nationalisation in 1948, the 7Fs were renumbered 53800-53810. Two of them (53809 and 53810) had had their larger diameter boilers replaced by standard, smaller diameter boilers in

1930, and the other three with the larger diameter boilers were similarly altered in 1953-55. Another 'bringing into line' involved the engines' tenders, the remaining 7-ton tenders being replaced by 5½-ton tenders. One of the replacement tenders was a 'hybrid', comprising a standard Fowler tank on a 1909 Deeley frame, this being attached to 53800 and later 53804. Apart from the reboilerings and the replacement tenders, the only significant alteration to which the 7Fs were subjected during the BR era was the fitting of Ferodo brake blocks. The Ferodo blocks had been experimentally fitted to 13801 in November 1943 and had given satisfaction. They weighed only 8lbs instead of the 51lbs of the cast iron blocks and, apart from having an estimated life five times that of cast iron, the Ferodo blocks eliminated the problem of dust which caused considerable wear to the crosshead and slide bars. The problem of braking on the gradients with the old-style cast iron blocks was entertainingly described by Colin Maggs in his *The Last Years of the Somerset & Dorset*. Maggs explains that S&D railwaymen simply didn't have the time between passenger trains to stop and pin down the brakes and then release them, one former driver having told him that, on occasions, a night

### SUMMARY OF S&D 7F 2-8-0s

| BR No. | Built | S&D No. | 1930 LMS No. | 1932 LMS No. | Date BR No. applied | Wdn. | Cut up at |
|---|---|---|---|---|---|---|---|
| 53800 | 2.1914 | 80 | 9670 | 13800 | 5.1948 | 6.1959 | Derby |
| 53801 | 3.1914 | 81 | 9671 | 13801 | 7.1949 | 6.1961 | Crewe |
| 53802 | 3.1914 | 82 | 9672 | 13802 | 6.1948 | 3.1960 | Doncaster |
| 53803 | 4.1914 | 83 | 9673 | 13803 | 4.1949 | 1.1962 | Crewe |
| 53804 | 4.1914 | 84 | 9674 | 13804 | 8.1948 | 1.1962 | Crewe |
| 53805 | 8.1914 | 85 | 9675 | 13805 | 11.1949 | 2.1961 | Crewe |
| 53806 | 7.1925 | 86 | 9676 | 13806 | 1.1950 | 1.1964 | Cashmore's, Newport |
| 53807 | 7.1925 | 87 | 9677 | 13807 | 4.1950 | 9.1964 | Cashmore's, Newport |
| 53808 | 7.1925 | 88 | 9678 | 13808 | 8.1949 | 3.1964 | Preserved |
| 53809 | 7.1925 | 89 | 9679 | 13809 | 9.1949 | 5.1964 | Preserved |
| 53810 | 8.1925 | 90 | 9680 | 13810 | 4.1949 | 11.1963 | Cashmore's, Newport |

S&D No.90 – which eventually became 53810 – shows off its large boiler while standing under the coal stage at Bath shed on 24 May 1929. The girder above the engine was used to convey tubs of coal to engines on adjoining roads. *Photograph: H.C.Casserley*

UK travelled by train, 27% by car and 26% by coach) the usual means of transportation for most people were the railways. Given that the S&D provided an important link between the Midlands and the ever-popular holiday resort of Bournemouth, on summer Saturdays the traffic on the line was intensive. This in itself put enough of a strain on the operating department, but there were other flies in the ointment, not least of all that the long-distance through trains were usually ten or more coaches and that most needed assistance over the steeply graded section between Evercreech Junction and Bath. Despite the availability of fairly modern types of locomotives such as Black Fives and, from 1951, Bulleid Pacifics, to meet the demands, Bath shed had only nine engines available to cover eight summer Saturday turns and, as that left negligible leeway in case of failures, virtually any engine that was available was prepared 'just in case'. And that included the 7Fs.

That the 7Fs were available for passenger duties was because the goods workings on the S&D on summer Saturday daytimes were virtually nil. As far as the 7Fs were concerned, their only diagrammed goods turns on Saturdays were late in the evening – i.e. after the passenger rush had died down. These duties were the 8.55pm Bath-Evercreech Junction and return and the 10.50pm Bath-Templecombe and return. The lack of goods workings during the daytime on summer Saturdays also helped to reduce congestion on the line, especially

shift at Evercreech could be like "Brock's Benefit Night, with fire and flames coming off the loco and tender wheels."

As a final word on the matter of modifications, 53804 suffered an unintentional customisation in September 1954 when it collided with a Black Five at Bath shed and lost part of its motion. Despite fears that 53804 might be withdrawn, it was repaired at Derby and performed another 7½ years' service on the S&D.

During the BR era the 7Fs' regular duties were pretty much the same as what had gone before. The mainstay was freight workings on the northern section of the S&D; for this, they were allowed a maximum of 17 loaded mineral wagons or 40 empties (or lightly loaded goods wagons) unaided between Bath and Evercreech. However, while that was what the engines did day in, day out, for most of the year, things were usually very different on summer Saturdays. By the early 1950s the nation's holiday habits were returning to normal, and as those were the days before mass car-ownership (in 1951 the British Tourist Association found that 47% of people taking a holiday in the

As noted in the text, the five 7Fs built in 1925 were fitted with larger diameter non-standard boilers. This angle gives a good view of one of these – the difference in size is very apparent. As 53807, this engine was refitted with one of the standard (smaller diameter) boilers in 1954. This picture was taken at Bath on 5 July 1947. *Photograph: H.C.Casserley*

Sporting a smaller diameter boiler of the same type as that with which it had been built in 1914, 13801 takes on water prior to turning at Templecombe on 6 July 1938. This engine later became 53801. *Photograph: H.C.Casserley*

as the single-line sections south of Templecombe could cause bottlenecks.

The activities of the 7Fs were regularly reported in the contemporary railway press. For example, in the summer of 1953 it was reported that they '...have again been prominent on Saturday expresses; as many as five in one day have been noted, and on more than one occasion one has made two double-trips from Bath to Bournemouth in a day'. In the summer of 1954 the reports noted that '...the 7Fs have again been out in great strength and no fewer than eight of the eleven were observed on passenger trains on 31 July'. This was fairly typical for the period.

For passenger duties the maximum loading for the 7Fs was 310 tons unassisted from Bath to Masbury (compared to 270 tons for Black Fives and Bulleids). They acquitted themselves well on passenger duties, speeds of up to 50mph being recorded but, with hindsight, it was later suggested that the engines' outings on this type of work did little for their long-term mechanical well-being and, consequently, hastened their eventual demise. The 7Fs were also often used on pigeon specials which had originated in the West Midlands. The specials ran every Friday during the summer and returned empty the following evening. The most popular release point for the birds was Templecombe.

In the other direction, the 7Fs were fairly regularly used north-westwards from Bath to Westerleigh Yard, Avonmouth and Stapleton Road Gas Works. But as in LMS days, they rarely

13801 under the coal stage at Bath, 4 July 1947. *Photograph: H.C.Casserley*

**53807 pulls away from Wellow with a lengthy Up goods on 6 July 1959.** *Photograph: R.C.Riley; www.transporttreasury.co.uk*

ventured any farther northwards than that, any sightings north of Westerleigh being usually accounted for by trips to/ from Derby Works. Perhaps the most celebrated foray – that of 53801 piloting the northbound *Pines Express* all the way to Birmingham on 26 September 1953 – was one of those which was tied in with a works visit, the engine being on its way to Derby for overhaul. Among the few recorded 'non-works' expeditions beyond Westerleigh involved 53805 which, on 28 December 1954, was observed heading for Birmingham with a train of fish wagons from the West Country.

The drafting of Standard Class 5 4-6-0s to the S&D in 1954 meant that there was less need to call on the 7Fs for heavy passenger work, though this was said to be 'more to the sorrow of photographers than passengers or the operating department'. However, the 7Fs reappeared on express passenger work in 1957 and 1958. In the latter year the first Saturday of the summer timetables (14 June) saw 53810 taking the 7.35am from Nottingham on from Bath to Bournemouth, deputising for the usual Bulleid Pacific. Other 7Fs appeared on most other Saturdays during that summer 'often with commendable

punctuality', as one observer reported. The first of the 7Fs to be withdrawn was 53800. It was dispatched to Derby in June 1959 for attention to the frames but the condition of the frames was such that the engine was promptly condemned. However, it was not cut up until the following January. 53802 was withdrawn in February 1960 and two others (53805 and 53810) were in store at Bath, but the other seven remained active for a little longer.

Perhaps surprisingly, the arrival of 9F 2-10-0s on the S&D for the summer of 1960 did not result in the 7Fs being eclipsed. They were seen in strength on passenger workings on the line throughout the summer, often being seen on the 7.00am Templecombe-Bath local (usually a 4F turn), the Sidmouth/ Exeter-Cleethorpes in both directions, and the 11.55am ex-Bath (the 9.08am Birmingham New St-Bournemouth).

Nevertheless, withdrawals resumed in February 1961 when 53805 made its final trip to Derby. The following month it was sent to Crewe for cutting up. In June 1961 it was decided that 53801 should not have its requisite overhaul, but should be taken out of service instead. It left Bath on 21 June but was held at Saltley for a couple of months

before being forwarded to Crewe for scrapping. The reduction of the class to seven in number made little difference to their 'summer Saturday' activities as, during the summer of 1961, they were regularly used on passenger trains. Among the numerous sightings that summer were those of 53809 in charge of the 11.12am Bournemouth West-Sheffield on 8 July, 53810 on the 11.12am Bournemouth-Sheffield on 26 August and 53807 on the Exmouth-Cleethorpes on the same day.

53803 and 53804 were withdrawn in January 1962, which meant that only the five 1925-built engines, 53806-53810, were left in service. During the summer of 1962, 53806 and 53807 were noted on specials from Bath on 28 July (10.23am and 9.29am respectively), and on that same day 53808 worked the 12.25pm Bath-Bournemouth West (7.35am ex-Nottingham) while 53810 arrived without a pilot at Bath on the Exmouth-Cleethorpes through train. The Exmouth-Cleethorpes was in fact a fairly regular job for the 7Fs that summer – they took over at Templecombe. The last 'Cleethorpes' that summer was on Saturday 8 September, the northbound train being formed of eight coaches and headed by

53808. It had to stop for a blow up at Shepton Mallet but ran from there to Bath in just 40 minutes, passing Masbury summit at 24mph. Not bad for a 37-year-old freight engine!

By 1962 the regular goods duties of the surviving engines included the 3.30am Bath-Evercreech Junction, 5.00am Bath-Evercreech and return, the 5.30am to Westerleigh and Stapleton Road (and a similar trip in the afternoons), 8.55am coal empties to Midsomer Norton and return with loaded coal wagons, 11.10am Bath-Evercreech Junction and 1.45pm return, and the 6.27pm to Avonmouth.

Successful trials with 8F 2-8-0s in 1963 paved the way for the gradual withdrawal of the remaining five engines. By the end of May 1964 only 53807 and 53809 were left and, as a tribute to these charismatic engines, it was intended to use both survivors on a special train from Bournemouth to Bath on 7 June. A fortnight before the trip, 53807 was sent to Swindon for minor repairs in order to be fit for the journey. This was probably the first – and most definitely the last – time one of the S&D 7Fs had visited Swindon. Unfortunately for enthusiasts, plans for the 7F double-header were scuppered by the withdrawal of the other engine, 53809, on 30 May, so 4F 0-6-0 44558 deputised.

The withdrawal of 53809 meant that 53807 was left as the last S&D 7F in BR service. However, that status came to an end in September 1964 when it, too, was withdrawn.

**Preservation**
All five of the 7Fs which were withdrawn in 1963/64 were sold to private scrap dealers. Of those, 53808 and 53809 went to Dai Woodham's at Barry from where, famously, no less than 213 still-intact locomotives were eventually rescued by preservationists. 53808 was one of those to be saved. It was purchased from Woodham's in October 1975 by the Somerset & Dorset Railway Trust and was restored to working order. It now lives on the West Somerset Railway and currently runs as S&D No.88, complete with a superb Prussian Blue livery. 53809 was also saved. It was purchased from Woodham's in December 1975 and was also restored. It is now based at the Midland Railway Centre at Butterley, Derbyshire, but over the years it has performed on various preserved lines all over Britain. In 2006 it was on the West Somerset Railway in the company of S&D No.88, and in October 2007 it was on the Avon Valley Railway at Bitton on the ex-Midland Railway Bath-Bristol line – a line which the 7Fs routinely worked with freights from Bath to Westerleigh and Avonmouth. Less well-known is the fact that the former tender of 53805 also survives; it is attached to one of Britain's most historic engines of the 20th century – the first Midland Compound 4-4-0, No.1000, which is at the National Railway Museum at York.

*Note: This feature is based on an article which appeared in* British Railways Illustrated Vol.4 No.9. *Much of the material was gathered from engine history sheets and S&D and LMS minute books, which were sourced at The National Archives at Kew. Other material was gleaned from the excellent booklet* The Somerset & Dorset 2-8-0s *by D.Milton (published by the Somerset and Dorset Railway Museum Trust) and various contemporary periodicals, particularly the* Railway Observer.

# ABOARD A 7F
*The late R.C.Riley – several of whose photographs appear in this series of books – rode on the footplate of 7F 53810 in June 1962. He wrote about the trip in the December 1962 edition of* Railway World; *the text is reproduced here with permission.*

My journey was made on the 11.10am to Evercreech Junction on 53810 which had been working for over four years since its last general overhaul and had not visited the shops since. Bearing in mind the heavy nature of the daily duties of the 7Fs this was a creditable record. It had already worked the 3.50am freight to Clifton Bridge, with coal for Portishead power station, returning with freight from Westerleigh. 53810 came off Bath shed at 10.55 and stood in the siding beside the gas works. A pannier tank – the only sign of the new regime at Bath Green Park – shunted the train out of the yard a few minutes later into a position for 53810 to couple on. There was a brief delay waiting for 8F 48660 with 15 loaded wagons to come off the 'Dorset' into the down road, into a position to propel its train to the down sidings. 53810 backed on to its own train and the guard of the coal train changed over to our train with no chance of a breather.

As soon as the dummy came off, the driver gave three crows on the whistle, the pannier tank at the rear responded, and both engines were opened up at once, hard at it right from the start to tackle the 1 in 50 climb to Devonshire Tunnel. The tablet catcher was pushed out, the pouch collected, drawn in again and safely stowed away. Our load was 20 wagons, and an outside observer, Mr.Ivo Peters, who had photographed us near the tunnel mouth, considered that we made an unusually fast climb of the bank. Devonshire Tunnel is not particularly long; we emerged briefly, and then entered Combe Down Tunnel, just over a mile in length. The gradient changes about 50 yards inside the tunnel and, at the tunnel mouth, the banker ceased its efforts and returned light to Bath, surrendering the 'Bath Bank Engine' staff at the Junction box. Once over the summit, 53810's regulator was shut and we coasted down the hill towards Midford. The fire was kept high throughout and there was always plenty of steam. In spite of its high mileage the engine rode well, the only fault being a slight knock in one of the rear boxes.

53810 was opened up again through Midford Station, where the tablet was surrendered, for the double track section commences on the viaduct over the closed GWR Camerton branch. Over the next six miles or so through Wellow to Radstock the gradients changed frequently and in the brake van the guard was busily adjusting the hand brake to hold the train in check. At Radstock North the calling-on arm was off, indicating to the driver that he could pull up to the platform but that the level crossing gates would be closed. Here I missed the once familiar sight of one of the two curious little S&D four-wheeled Sentinel locomotives, built to reduced loading gauge to pass under the bridge behind the signalbox. The last Sentinel had been withdrawn a few months earlier and the bridge demolished to allow a 3F 0-6-0 tank to pass freely into the wagon works beyond. One of these engines, 47557, came on to the rear of the train and in the normal way would be coupled in order to bank us on the formidable climb of the Mendips to Masbury summit, nearly eight miles, much of it at 1 in 50. But on this occasion, we were banked only as far as Midsomer Norton where we had to set back eight empty wagons into Norton Hill Colliery sidings. This job would normally have been carried out by the 12.35pm from Bath, which had been cancelled on this day.

The reduced load required no banking assistance, nor did the engine need to be worked hard for the rest of the outward journey. Had a banker been provided it would have collected a wrong line staff at Binegar, permitting it to run back light from the summit on the down road, crossing to the up road at Binegar. At some point between Binegar and the summit the guard would uncouple the banking engine by means of the hook provided for the purpose on the smokebox door handrail. Latterly the hooks were seldom used as the guard could not reach it from the BR standard brake van and would use a shunter's pole instead. Once over the summit we coasted down to Shepton Mallet with regular brake applications to keep the train in check.

We paused for 6 minutes to take water and were away again soon after 12.30. The fire was burning through now, but there was an easy task ahead, a brief climb out of the station and then falling gradients all the way to Evercreech Junction. Strangely enough, the driver had not previously encountered Mr.Peters and it was always interesting to speculate where he would appear next; I believe he photographed us six times on the down run!

Although the 7Fs spent almost all of their working lives on the S&D, it was fairly common to see one working in the other direction from Bath – to Westerleigh Yard, Avonmouth and Stapleton Road Gas Works. This is 53809 coming off the Avonmouth line and joining the LMS main line at Kingswood Junction in Bristol on 9 May 1964. One assumes that the train is heading back to Bath, in which case it will leave the main line Mangotsfield and take the branch through Warmley, Bitton, Kelston and Weston. *Photograph: Eric Ashton Collection*

At Evercreech Junction we came to a stand with the whole train clear of the Highbridge branch tracks. Then one of the tall lattice post shunt signals, peculiar to the S&D, was cleared and 53810 propelled its train back into the sidings alongside the branch. There was nearly an hour to allow the engine to be turned and the fire made ready for the return journey.

We set off again towards Bath at 1.45pm with a load of 24, and made a good climb to Masbury without assistance, which is not normally required for the loads in the up direction, although a good part of the climb is at 1 in 50 and 1 in 55 against the engine. At Midsomer Norton we stopped to detach 20 empties and the 0-6-0 tank which came on the rear to take the wagons required our assistance to get its load into the station before shunting the wagons into the colliery sidings. In their place we took on 14 loaded coal wagons, small coal for power station use. Down the hill into Radstock the distinctive smell of the brake linings was apparent. Throughout much of the journey, apart from the worst banks, both uphill and downhill speeds were more or less uniform at about 25 to 30mph.

At Radstock we took on eight wagons and our train now consisted of:

2 wagons peat, Ashcott-Bristol.
1 container, Glastonbury-Bristol.
5 vans, empty ex-Radstock repair works.
1 wagon coal, Radstock Colliery-Radstock West (via Bath, Bristol and Wells!)
2 wagons coal, Writhlington Colliery-CEGB Portishead.
14 wagons coal, Norton Hill Colliery- CEGB Portishead.
1 Brake van.

The load was therefore 26 actual wagons; allowing 'equal 1½' for a 13-ton coal wagon and 'equal 2' for a 16-ton coal wagon the load was calculated as 'equal 39', the maximum summer load. ('Equal 36' is the permitted maximum in winter months.)

We were soon away again and the reason for the early start from Evercreech Junction and brisk working subsequently soon became apparent. A cautious approach was made to the summit after Wellow and brakes were applied in readiness for the single line section. Our luck was out, however, and Midford outer home signal remained resolutely on. This signal had been resited about 200yd back in recent years because of difficulties experienced in stopping heavy loose-coupled freight trains at this point. The fireman quickly went to the telephone but we were not in time to be admitted to the single line

section without running the risk of delaying the 'Pines Express'. There followed a 25-minute wait for the express to pass, and a further 12 minutes for a stopping passenger train. At 3.37pm, nearly 40 minutes after reaching the outer home, the signal came off. The driver opened up 53810 immediately to take advantage of the short stretch of falling gradient and get a run at the bank. By the time we reached Midford goods yard the regulator was fully open and the strident exhaust beats of the engine resounded across the hills as we tackled the last climb up to Combe Down Tunnel. It was the single bore of this tunnel that brought about 89's accident in 1929, when the crew were overcome by fumes, and engine and train ran down the bank to Bath out of control. Inevitably with the full load on this 1 in 50 gradient 53810 needed to be worked hard, but in spite of the recent passage of two other trains the fumes in the tunnel were not particularly bad. As soon as we emerged from the tunnel the hard work was over, the regulator was closed and the driver's hand moved to the brake handle to control the speed of the train on the run down the bank.

# Evercreech Junction

This picture looks north-west from the footbridge at the Down end of Evercreech Junction – the divergence of the Burnham and Bath lines is just out of view around the bend in the distance. A train for Bath stands at the Up platform. The engine and two coaches on the centre road are the Highbridge branch train; as the station had only two platforms the branch train had to vacate the platform between journeys. The centre road was also used to accommodate the pilot engines which were needed to help the heaviest trains up to Masbury Summit. This picture was taken on 22 July 1958. *Photograph: R.C.Riley; www.transporttreasury.co.uk*

*Left.* The legendary Evercreech Junction – a favourite of the late Sir John Betjeman – did not start life as a junction. When it opened to the public on 3 February 1862 it was merely a small wayside station on the Somerset Central Railway's line from Burnham to Cole. The Somerset Central amalgamated with the Dorset Central in 1862 to form the S&D and in July 1874 the S&D opened the 'Bath Extension' which diverged from the original Somerset Central line a couple of hundred yards beyond the north-west end of Evercreech station. Thus the station became Evercreech Junction. Here, veteran 3F 43682 crosses the A371 road immediately beyond the south end of the station with a Templecombe to Burnham-on-Sea excursion on Wednesday 12 July 1961. Although Burnham had lost its ordinary passenger services in 1951 it continued to accommodate the occasional excursion or special working until September 1962. The train in our picture was in fact an ordinary service train (the 12.00 noon from Templecombe) which was advertised in the timetables to run only as far as Highbridge, but on Wednesdays and Saturdays during the summer was extended to Burnham. *Photograph: Peter Barnfield*

*Below.* 9F 92220 *Evening Star* pulls across to the Down platform at Evercreech Junction with empty stock on 7 September 1963. Of all the 251 9Fs, *Evening Star* was of course the best-known, having been the very last steam locomotive to be built for British Railways. Built at Swindon at a cost of £33,500, it was painted in lined green livery, complete with copper capped chimney for which Swindon locomotives were recognised the world over. The other 250 9Fs spent all their lives painted plain black. 92220 was also the only one of the class to be named, the name being decided through a competition. Three entrants – all Western Region workers – suggested the name *Evening Star*. Although the loco was something of a celebrity, that seems to have counted for nothing in 1962 as, when it first came to Bath shed in August of that year, it was in a very shabby condition. *Evening Star* spent only a couple of months at Bath in 1962 but, as this picture confirms, it returned for the late summer of 1963. *Evening Star's* working life on BR lasted for only five years – it entered traffic in March 1960 and was withdrawn in March 1965. Such foresight! Given *Evening Star's* place in the history of British steam locomotive development it was unsurprising that it was saved for preservation. It is now part of the National Railway Museum collection and, in the past forty-two years, has been used on a number of 'main line' steam specials all over the country and has also appeared on various preserved lines. Forty-two years in preservation – yes, that is more than eight times longer that the loco's life with BR. *Photograph: David Idle; www.transporttreasury.co.uk*

Class 4 4-6-0 75072 enters Evercreech Junction with an Up train on a damp and thoroughly dismal-looking day in October 1956, just a few months into its S&D life. Along with classmates 75070 and 75071, 75072 had been transferred from Exmouth Junction to Bath shed in May 1956. Of those three, 75070 was replaced by 75073 in March 1957, and the new threesome (75071, 75072 and 75073) were to remain at Bath until November 1962, when they were all transferred to Templecombe. They departed from Templecombe one by one during 1964 and 1965. We will be seeing several other Class 4s elsewhere in this book, and also in other books in this series, but most of the others will be seen with 3,500-gallon tenders. 75072 was different. It was one of fifteen (75065-75079) which were paired with high-sided 4,725-gallon tenders; these fifteen were built for use on the Southern Region, where there were no water troughs. *Photograph: Derek Clayton*

4F 0-6-0 44523 removes three brake vans from the rear of a goods train at the north-west end of Evercreech Junction on 26 September 1959. *Three* brake vans on a goods train? Yes – they were the mode of conveyance for members of the Bath Railway Society, the vans being attached to the rear of an ordinary goods train for a trip from Bath to Evercreech Junction and back. Immediately beyond the engine the Bath line curves round to the right; the original Somerset Central line to Highbridge and Burnham continues into the distance. *Photograph: Hugh Ballantyne*

3F 43216 poodles into Evercreech Junction with the 4.00pm from Highbridge on Tuesday 22 July 1958. 3Fs had been built for the S&D – five in 1896 and five more in 1902 – but some of those native engines were later transferred away while others came in from elsewhere. 43216 was one of the natives, having been built for the S&D in 1902. In the mid-1950s it and the S&D's other 3Fs had some of their regular duties taken over by 4Fs and Ivatt 2-6-2Ts which had themselves been ousted from main line duties by Standard 2-6-0s and 4-6-0s. Subsequently, the 3Fs were used mainly on the Highbridge branch. Nevertheless, they proved to be remarkably tenacious and a couple remained on the S&D – allocated to Templecombe – until 1962. 43216 was withdrawn in August 1962; of the ten 3Fs which had been built specially for the S&D it was the last to survive. Moreover, by the latter part of 1962 it had become one of the very last survivors of the once-numerous class anywhere in Britain. The engine is not the only point of interest in this picture; just look at the smashing little shunting signal in the left foreground. *Photograph: R.C.Riley; www.transporttreasury.co.uk*

When the S&D's celebrated 'Bath Extension' opened in 1874 it became the main line. This meant that the Evercreech Junction-Burnham section of the original main line was relegated to the status of a branch. Here, Ivatt 2-6-2T 41296 has just left Evercreech Junction with the 5.00pm 'branch train' to Highbridge. The signalman at North box waits to give the staff to the driver. *Photograph: R.C.Riley; www.transporttreasury.co.uk*

# Templecombe

7F 53805 heads north on the S&D main line at Templecombe on 9 July 1960. It is passing the shed yard. One of the two tracks continuing from the shed yard and passing under the road bridge in the distance on the left used to connect with the SR main line ¼-mile or so to the east of Templecombe Upper station; the connection was opened in 1862 and was used by shuttle services between the S&D station and the L&SWR station, but it was abandoned in 1870 following the opening of the new direct connection between the S&D and the Templecombe Upper. Turning our attention back to the locomotive, we can see that its Whitaker tablet apparatus is extended – this is the 'bar' protruding from the side of the tender. For a closer look at this apparatus see page 56. *Photograph: J.A.C.Kirke; www.transporttreasury.co.uk*

Templecombe shed nestled beneath the embankment which took a minor lane to the hamlet of Combe Throop over the railway, and the embankment and the adjacent road bridge offered a good vantage point for photography. The picture is undated, but the presence of WR Pannier Tank 4691 confirms it is no earlier than February 1961 as that is when that loco was transferred to Templecombe. The shed had seen its first Pannier Tank in late 1958 when one had arrived for trials, but the first to be permanently allocated there was 9651, which was transferred from Wrexham in January 1959. In March 1959 it was replaced by 3765, which was itself replaced by 3720 in September of that same year. Apparently, the locos had to have their steps and ATC gear altered before they could be used on the S&D. Behind the Pannier Tank in our picture is 2P 40564, a very long-standing resident of Templecombe shed. *Photograph: Paul Chancellor Collection.*

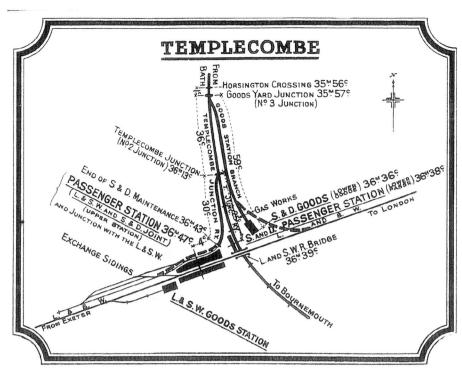

TEMPLECOMBE

Horsington Crossing 35ᴹ 56ᶜ
Goods Yard Junction 35ᴹ 57ᶜ
(Nº 3 Junction)

Templecombe Junction
(Nº 2 Junction) 36ᴹ 13ᶜ

End of S & D Maintenance 36ᴹ 40ᶜ

PASSENGER STATION 36ᴹ 47ᶜ
(L. & S.W. AND S & D. JOINT)
(UPPER STATION)
AND JUNCTION WITH THE L. & S.W.

EXCHANGE SIDINGS

Gas Works

S. & D. GOODS (LOWER GOODS) 36ᴹ 36ᶜ

S. AND D. PASSENGER STATION (LOWER PASSR.) 36ᴹ 38ᶜ
L. AND S. W.

To London

L. AND S.W.R. BRIDGE 36ᴹ 39ᶜ

To Bournemouth

L. & S.W. GOODS STATION

From Exeter

The arrangements for S&D trains calling at Templecombe were awkward, and will be described in detail in one of the other books in this series. But as a taster of what is to come, here is 9F 92224 at the rear of the 9.03am Bristol-Bournemouth West as it is being reversed away from the S&D platform at the 'main line' station (Templecombe Upper) on 7 September 1963. There is another engine hauling at the far end of the train; when the train has reached the junction with the running line (a little under ½-mile to the north of the station), this will leave 92224 at the front of the train, facing south and ready to continue to Bournemouth. Whereas the line had been double track all the way from Midford, at Templecombe Junction it reverted to single track and, apart from an eight-mile long section of double track between Blandford and Corfe Mullen and the provision of passing places at some of the other intermediate stations, it was single for the rest of the way to Broadstone Junction. *Photograph: David Idle; www.transporttreasury.co.uk*

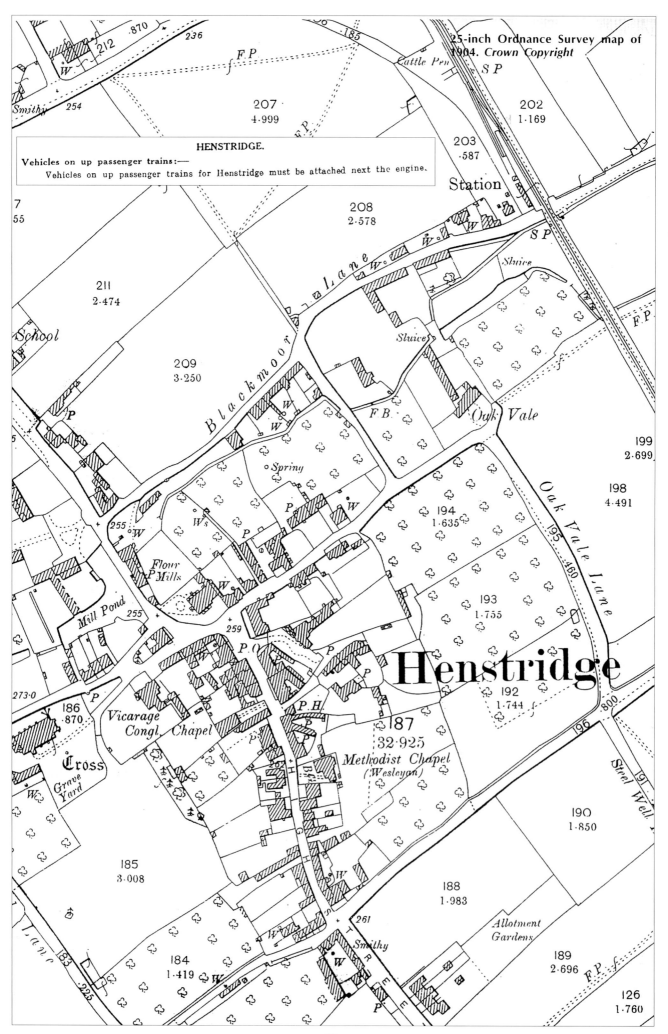

25-inch Ordnance Survey map of 1904. Crown Copyright

**HENSTRIDGE.**

**Vehicles on up passenger trains:—**
 Vehicles on up passenger trains for Henstridge must be attached next the engine.

Station

Henstridge

**S&D Joint Committee minutes, 2 February 1944**

5194

**HENSTRIDGE:**
**ENLARGEMENT OF PARCELS OFFICE**

It was recommended by Joint Conference minute No.1080 that confirmation be given to the arrangements which had been made for the parcels office at Henstridge to be enlarged, as indicated on plan No.10/2289.G./P.4 submitted, at a cost of £68 : 14 : 1, in order to provide adequate accommodation for the additional parcels traffic now being dealt with at that Station.

Confirmed.

# Henstridge

Continuing our journey south on the S&D, the last station in Somerset was at Henstridge. If platform length were the only measure of a station's size, Henstridge, with a platform of just 150ft, was the smallest station on the entire S&D main line. The village it served had a population of 1,050 (1951 census). Maxwell Fraser's *Somerset Ways* (published by the GWR [sorry!] in 1934) notes that the village '...has a church which is chiefly notable for a 15th century altar tomb. The Virginia Inn at the crossroads *(the junction of the A30 and A357)* was once a famous coaching house. It is said to be the place where Sir Walter Raleigh's servant emptied a stoup of beer over his master, who was smoking, in the belief that he was on fire'. That story is well-known, but it should be borne in mind that Sherborne Castle also claims to be the place where the incident occurred. This delightful picture was taken on 4 July 1961. We are looking north-westwards towards Templecombe. Some of the station's modest goods facilities – a pair of sidings, a 1-ton hand crane, cattle pens and a milk dock – can be seen beyond the platform. The photographer is standing on the level crossing which took Blackmoor Lane across the railway. The crossing gates were hand-operated but were locked by one of the levers of the 10-lever ground frame which was in the station building. *Photograph: R.C.Riley; www.transporttreasury.co.uk*

S&D Joint Committee minutes, 20 July 1932

## PARISH OF HENSTRIDGE
### PROPOSED EXTENSION OF CHURCHYARD

The Rating Agent reported that an application had been made to the Joint Committee by the Vicar of Henstridge (The Rev. B. W. Shepheard-Walwyn) for assistance towards the cost of extending the Churchyard, which is practically full.

In order to obviate the adoption of the Burial Acts and provision of a Public Cemetery estimated to cost £1,000 with a consequent Burial Rate in perpetuity it is proposed to extend the existing Churchyard by including an additional 1 r. 35 p. of ground which the Vicar is giving from the Glebe land, estimated to suffice for 30 years on the present basis of population. The last addition to the Churchyard was made in 1905, 34 perches of land then being added.

It is stated by the Vicar that there is only one large landowner in the Parish, Miss Guest, who has promised to contribute the sum of £50 towards the cost of the scheme, in addition to which Mr. A. W. James, who owns his own farm, is providing the stone for walling at cost price and will also probably make a contribution.

The cost of extension, including the laying out of the new ground, walls, fences, paths, conveyance, consecration, etc., is estimated at £225. The total Rateable Value of the Parish is £4,016 and the Joint Committee's Rateable Value £108, or 2.69 per cent., their proportion of the cost of the extension being £6 : 1s : - in addition to which a payment would have to be made to the Railway Rebates Fund in the event of the cost of providing further burial accommodation becoming a charge on the local rates.

Assuming that an annual rate of 3d. in the £ were required to provide a Public Burial Ground in the Parish the Joint Committee's payment on the basis of their present assessment would amount to £1 : 7s : - to the Local Authority and £3 : 7 : 9 to the Railway Rebates Fund, or a total of £4 : 14 : 9 per annum.

In the circumstances it is recommended, with the approval of the Managements that the Joint Committee contribute the sum of £10 towards the cost of the proposed extension on the conditions that the total sum required is subscribed and the scheme carried out by voluntary effort.

Recommendation approved.

*Top right.* An estate car – it looks like an Austin A70 – and a Land Rover wait while a Down train leaves Stalbridge on 16 September 1963. The LSWR-type signal box adjacent to the crossing was erected in 1903 to replace the original 'box. It had 18 levers and the wheel for the crossing gates. *Photograph: P.Gomm; www.transporttreasury.co.uk*

*Bottom right.* A familiar feature of Sturminster Newton was the smashing little timber-built 16-lever signal box at the end of the Up platform. This picture was taken on 4 July 1961. Beautiful! *Photograph: R.C.Riley; www.transporttreasury.co.uk*

*Below.* Ivatt 2-6-2T 41208 prepares to pull away from Henstridge with the 12.23pm Templecombe-Bournemouth West on 29 March 1965. The accompanying Ordnance Survey map shows that the station was on the fringe of the town, access being along Blackmoor Lane. The map is actually a little deceptive; it makes Blackmoor Lane seem like a decent-size thoroughfare but, in fact, it is a very narrow little lane which peters out into an unmade track immediately past the site of the station. The site of the station is still discernible today, though the only remaining railway infrastructure is the concrete posts from which the level crossing gates once hung. Short sections of the old trackbed on both sides of the crossing are walkable. *Photograph: Paul Strong*

# North Dorset signal boxes

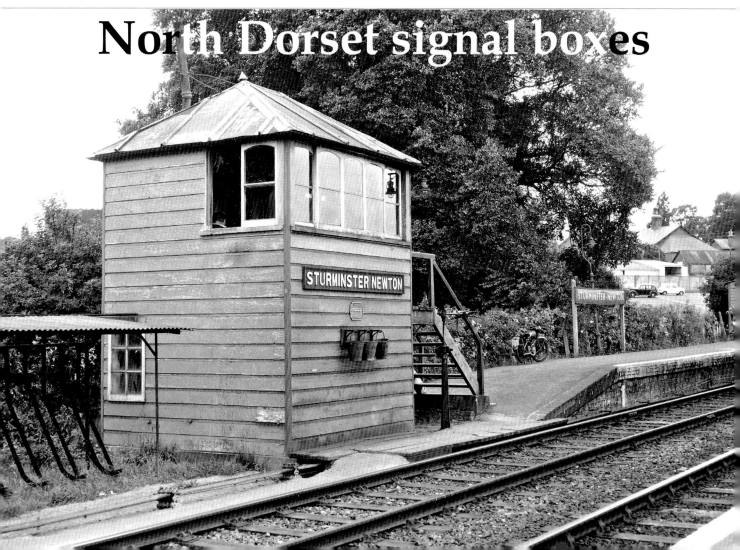

# Blandford Forum

*Above.* BR Class 3 2-6-2T 82039 pulls away from Blandford Forum with a local for Bournemouth West on 10 July 1959. The station spent most of its life as plain old 'Blandford', the 'Forum' not being added until 21 September 1953. The *Tourists' Descriptive Guide to the Somerset & Dorset Railway* of 1874 commented that '...the town contains several fine streets, and for a country town the general architecture is superior, and a thoroughly well-to-do aspect pervades the place... In 1731 a great fire causing immense destruction of property and sad loss of life occurred, hence in some measure the handsome and modern character of the existing buildings, almost all of which are brick... The railway station is one of the busiest on the line, the requirements for the trade of the town and a large thriving agricultural district being here concentrated.' *Photograph: R.C.Riley; www.transporttreasury.co.uk*

*Below.* Class 4 2-6-0 76011 waits with a Down train at Blandford Forum on a bright, sunny day in February 1966. Although most of the S&D closed completely the following month, Blandford subsequently accommodated a number of special passenger workings. The very last of these was an excursion to Kew on 15 June 1968; it called at the closed stations of Bailey Gate and Broadstone, one of the conditions for the trip being that passengers boarding at the disused stations did so entirely at their own risk. The return train from Waterloo went only to Bournemouth as, by that time, trains were permitted on the S&D only during hours of daylight. Blandford's ability to host special trains after 'closure' in 1966 was because the line southwards from there to Broadstone had been kept open for goods and milk traffic. That section did not officially close until Monday 6 January 1969; latterly it had been worked as a siding from Broadstone. *Photograph: Peter Barnfield*

This view of a 'train-less' Blandford Forum station on 4 July 1961 provides a good uncluttered view of the buildings. The railings below the far end of the Down (right-hand) platform canopy guard the steps to the subway which linked the two platforms. Blandford was the only station on the S&D to have a subway. Another idiosyncrasy was that the subway was diagonal: on the Up (left-hand) platform access was at the near end of the canopy. *Photograph: R.C.Riley; www.transporttreasury.co.uk*

This 'carriage window' picture looks across to the Down platform at Blandford Forum, with the goods yard behind. The signal box had been built in 1893 to replace the previous box which had been damaged by fire. However, the new 'box soon proved to be accident-prone as well, as in 1906 it was struck by lightning and caught fire. It had to be substantially reconstructed, and in its final form it had 27 levers. Before moving to our next picture, the Irwell Press Health & Safety Consultant, Mr.Humphrey Hardhat, takes us to task over this photograph. He says we should not be seen to be endorsing 'carriage window' pictures – leaning out of carriage window is most definitely in the 'no' category. He adds that it makes no difference whether one has a camera or not; one might finish up not only minus camera, but also minus head. *Photograph: Paul Chancellor Collection*

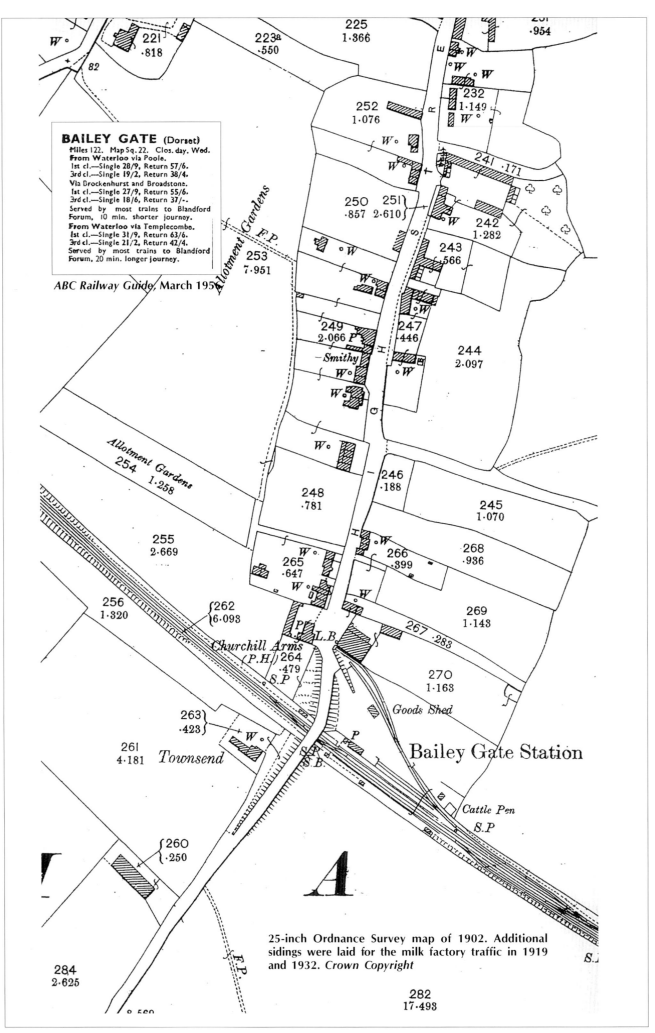

**BAILEY GATE** (Dorset)
Miles 122. Map Sq. 22. Clos. day. Wed.
**From Waterloo via Poole.**
1st cl.—Single 28/9, Return 57/6.
3rd cl.—Single 19/2, Return 38/4.
Via Brockenhurst and Broadstone.
1st cl.—Single 27/9, Return 55/6.
3rd cl.—Single 18/6, Return 37/-.
Served by most trains to Blandford
Forum, 10 min. shorter journey.
**From Waterloo via Templecombe.**
1st cl.—Single 31/9, Return 63/6.
3rd cl.—Single 21/2, Return 42/4.
Served by most trains to Blandford
Forum, 20 min. longer journey.

*ABC Railway Guide,* March 1956

221
.818

223ª
.550

225
1·366

·954

232
1·149

252
1·076

241 ·171

250
·857

251
2·610

242
1·282

243
·566

*Allotment Gardens* F.P.

253
7·951

249
2·066 P

247
·446

244
2·097

— *Smithy*

*Allotment Gardens*
254 1·258

248
·781

246
·188

245
1·070

255
2·669

265
·647

266
·399

268
·936

256
1·320

262
6·093

269
1·143

267 ·283

*Churchill Arms*
(P.H) 264
·479
S.P

L.B.

270
1·163

*Goods Shed*

263
·423

261
4·181 *Townsend*

**Bailey Gate Station**

S.P
L.B.

P

*Cattle Pen*
S.P

260
·250

𝐴

284
2·625

F.P.

25-inch Ordnance Survey map of 1902. Additional
sidings were laid for the milk factory traffic in 1919
and 1932. *Crown Copyright*

282
17·493

S.

# Bailey Gate

4F 0-6-0 44557 of Templecombe shed pauses at Bailey Gate station on 4 July 1961. The train is the 7.00am Evercreech Junction-Poole goods, so the engine would be required to undertake whatever shunting was necessary at Bailey Gate. In this picture the engine has drawn forward to the signal box (out of view to the left); either the driver is waiting to be given details of the shunting required or the work has already been done and the train is waiting to continue to Poole. Until the opening of Corfe Mullen halt in July 1929, Bailey Gate was the last station on the S&D 'proper' before it joined the LSWR at Wimborne and Broadstone. Despite its title, Bailey Gate was actually in the village of Sturminster Marshall. Indeed, until 1863 the station had been called Sturminster Marshall – the renaming was to avoid confusion with Sturminster Newton, 14½ miles to the north on the same stretch of railway. The line through Bailey Gate had originally been single, but was doubled northwards from here to Blandford in 1901 and southwards from here to Corfe Mullen in 1905. One item of interest is the hut on the left; it was used to store engineer's trolleys, these being run out on the rails and manually lifted on to the running line. We'll see more of these in other pictures elsewhere in this series. *Photograph: R.C.Riley; www.transporttreasury.co.uk*

## BAILEY GATE.

### Lake Crossing between Corfe Mullen Junction and Wimborne Junction :—

Before any train or engine passes over the crossing it must be brought to a stand clear of the gates when the guard working the train (or the fireman in case of light engine) must unlock the gates, place them across the roadway and take off the signal for the train (or engine) to pass.

When the train (or engine) has passed over the crossing, the guard (or fireman in the case of light engine) must place the signal to Danger and replace and lock the level crossing gates across the railway, taking the key to either Wimborne Junction or Corfe Mullen, as necessary.

Keys of the gates will be kept at Corfe Mullen and Wimborne Junction signal boxes. Down trains and light engines must stop at Corfe Mullen Junction, and up trains and light engines at Wimborne Junction to obtain same.

## BETWEEN BAILEY GATE AND WIMBORNE.

### Messrs. Carter & Co.'s Siding :—

This siding will be worked by guards of down trains running between Bailey Gate and Wimborne when instructed by the Station Master at Bailey Gate.

The train tablet must be used to release the lever frame.

*Top right.* Although Bailey Gate station was sparsely used by passengers, it dealt with a respectable amount of milk traffic from the factory on the north side of the station. This picture, which was taken from the bridge which took High Street over the railway at the north-west end of the station, was taken in February 1966. The milk factory dominates the background. The business was started in 1888 by a local farmer, Henry Tory. He was listed in the 1891 census as a Yeoman, living at No.15 Newton Marsh with his wife, two daughters, four sons (the eldest two, Henry Jⁿʳ and Clement, each being listed as 'assistant on farm'), Miss Ellen Squires ('general domestic servant'), Miss Helen Holloway ('housemaid – domestic') and Miss Emily Caines (listed as 'nurse – domestic', despite being only 14 years old). The mainstay of the business was making butter and cheese, but it also sold farm equipment and animal feedstuffs. The business developed to such an extent that, by the time of the Great War, the traffic warranted a milk train seven days a week; the train travelled empty from Templecombe and returned there with the full churns which were attached to an LSWR train for London. In 1910 the Tory family sold the business to Carters & Dorset Modern Dairies, and in 1918 it became part of United Dairies. At that time the business was still fairly small – it had a staff of ten and its delivery fleet comprised two solid-tyred motor vehicles. A new siding to the premises was laid in 1919. Although almost all of the S&D closed in March 1966, as we have already seen the section between Broadstone and Blandford Forum remained open for goods and milk traffic for almost three more years. When that section closed on 6 January 1969 it brought about the complete closure of the S&D south of Templecombe. The precise date of the last rail traffic from Bailey Gate seems to have gone unrecorded, but during the last few years it had been sparse. Latterly it had warranted only an 'as required' trip to and from Poole, usually worked by a 'Type 3' D65XX (Class 33) diesel.

The milk factory itself had expanded over the years and, by the 1950s, it had claimed to be the status of the largest Cheddar Cheese producing plant in the world and had had a staff of almost 300, some of whom lived in houses which had been built by the company. However, cheesemaking ceased in 1975 and the whey products division closed the following year, and the factory itself closed in 1978. Some packaging work remained, but that came to an end in 1989. *Photograph: Peter Barnfield*

Copy
R. 9307.

MINISTRY OF TRANSPORT,
4, Whitehall Gardens,
London, S.W.1.

24th June, 1932.

Sir,

I have the honour to report for the information of the Minister of Transport that, at the request of the Company's officers, I made an inspection on 21st June, 1932, of the new works at Bailey Gate Station on the Somerset and Dorset Joint Railway.

A new siding connection has been provided as a modification of an existing connection, trailing in the down line, to serve a depot of United Dairies, Limited. An additional shunt signal has also been provided for exit from the new connection.

The material of the new connection is 90 lb. serviceabl The new connection itself is suitably trapped but the laying of the new connection has in my opinion somewhat prejudiced the safe operation of the trap of the existing siding, and I suggested that it would be improved if the left hand rail of this trap were shortened by about 5 ft. so as to prevent a derailed vehicle being turned towards the running lines again by the outer rail of the new connection. The Company's officers agreed as to this and arranged for it to be done at once.

The siding is used for 3 or 4 milk tank wagons daily during the milk season and these are usually despatched to London via Templecombe.

The signal box contains an old frame of 24 levers of which 3 are Push and Pull, and 7 are spare. The altered locking is correct.

The works are complete and in good order and I recommend that they be approved.

I have the honour to be,
Sir,
Your obedient Servant,

(Signed) A.C. Trench.
Colonel.

Secretary,
Ministry of Transport.

*Below*. The milk traffic from Bailey Gate was taken out by a special train each afternoon – the 4.45pm to Templecombe. The engine and stock for that working were sent out from Templecombe as an ordinary 'public' passenger train – the 3.35pm to Bailey Gate. Although the 3.35's principal function was simply to get the engine and stock to Bailey Gate for the all-important milk train, it also provided a useful connection at Templecombe for passengers who had arrived on the 1.00pm ex-Waterloo and were bound for the North Dorset towns and villages. By the 1960s the motive power for the 3.35pm Templecombe-Bailey Gate and the 4.45pm milk train was often ex-GWR Pannier tank 4691 or, alternatively, a BR Class 3 2-6-2T. On 23 October 1965 the job fell to a Class 3, namely the positively filthy 82041 of Bath shed. It is seen standing 'wrong line' at Bailey Gate ready to depart with the milk train back to Templecombe. At Templecombe the milk vehicles were transferred to a 'main line' train and were taken to Vauxhall in south-west London. At Vauxhall the milk tankers were taken across to Platform 8 where they could discharge their contents into a bottling plant which was housed in one of the many brick arches under the railway. The dairy-related traffic at Bailey Gate was not all one way, as during the summer two 3,000-gallon tankers of whey arrived from Carmarthen each day. *Photograph: Hugh Ballantyne*

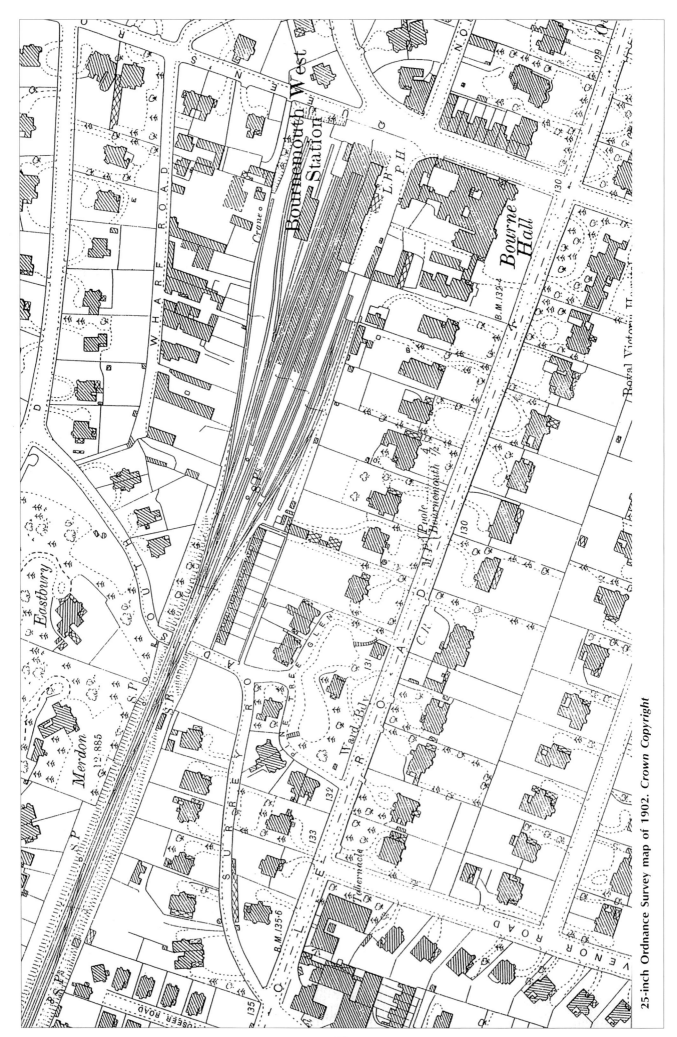

25-inch Ordnance Survey map of 1902. Crown Copyright

42

# Bournemouth West

Somerset & Dorset trains terminated, not in Dorset, but in Hampshire. The end of the journey was Bournemouth West station which was half a mile across the county border. Under the Local Government reforms of 1974 the town of Bournemouth was ceded to Dorset, but that was too late to have any effect on the S&D as it had closed eight years earlier. This picture of Bournemouth West, which looks towards the buffer stops of the almost train-free station, was taken on 27 May 1958. The station had been opened by the Poole & Bournemouth Railway (later part of the London & South Western) on 15 June 1874, the S&D's access being with the aid of running powers over the L&SWR and the P&B from Wimborne (later from Broadstone Junction). Bournemouth West was the original 'main line' station in the town, Bournemouth Central (as it was later known) not opening until 1885. The station had three double-sided platforms, but unlike many other terminus stations it had no cross-overs for engine release purposes. Somewhat ironically, the S&D's original target in the 1860s was not Bournemouth itself, but Poole, the railway being perceived as a connection between the ports of Burnham and Poole. That was, in turn, part of a larger scheme: there were already scheduled steamer services between Cardiff and Burnham (operated by the Cardiff Steam Navigation Company), so it was considered that, if steamer services were established between Poole and Cherbourg, the S&D would become an integral part of a through route between South Wales and mainland Europe. The Poole-Cherbourg service was operated by the S&D itself, using its own ships. In 1865 the S&D was advertising through journeys from Burnham and Cherbourg for a return fare of 15/- (1st Class) or 13/- (2nd Class). However, the Poole-Cherbourg service operated at a loss; it was suspended in 1867 and was never reinstated. This seemed to have put a dent in the S&D's ambitions for the southern part of its line but, fortuitously, nearby Bournemouth offered an invaluable alternative source of traffic. The Bournemouth traffic was, of course, due to the town's development as a holiday resort. In the early 1800s the Bournemouth area started to gain a reputation as a place of solitude for the well-heeled – the *very* well-heeled. Arguably, that trend had been set by Mary Elizabeth Bowes – then the richest heiress in England and an ancestor of the late Queen Mother – who had moved to Pokesdown in the 1790s to escape the clutches of her second husband. Although Bournemouth was still a small town, it was nevertheless upmarket – shops were prohibited in the town, so traders had to live outside (often in Poole or Christchurch) and travel in to make special calls. The notion of having nasty, dirty railways in the town was pooh-poohed by the citizens until the 1870s and, even then, the construction of a railway through the town was permitted only if it were largely in a deep cutting where it would be largely unseen. In common with many other sea-front towns all over the country, the coming of the railway turned Bournemouth into a very popular resort. The town grew – between 1880 and 1900 its population increased from 17,000 to 60,000 – but this was not all good news. The early property builders failed to provide adequate infrastructure – roads were poor and sewers insufficient – and it took the attentions of one Christopher Crabbe Creek (whose job title was – and we love this! – 'Surveyor of Nuisances for the Bournemouth Commissioners') to bring some order to the town's development. Largely as a result of Mr.Creek's attentions, in the late 1800s and early 1900s Bournemouth expanded at a remarkable rate, swallowing up Westbourne, Boscombe Spa and Southbourne-on-Sea which had, at one time, been competing resorts. This was, of course, very beneficial to the S&D – the Bournemouth traffic, although highly seasonal, became one of the railway's principal sources of revenue, a state of affairs that was retained until the early 1960s. Although trends come and go – and although the S&D no longer brings train-loads of holidaymakers to the South Coast – Bournemouth is still a very popular holiday resort today, especially among those who are looking for a slightly more genteel holiday rather than lots of loud music and flashing lights. The town is also a hugely popular location for retired people – it is, to a certain extent, the south-west's equivalent of Eastbourne. The town's not-inconsiderable population of, shall we say, the older age group has earned it the rather unkind nickname of 'GWR' – not Great Western Railway, but God's Waiting Room. *Photograph: Leslie Freeman; The Transport Treasury*

Class 4 4-6-0 73054 of Bath shed prepares to pull away from Bournemouth West with the 3.40pm to Bristol on 16 March 1963. Even though this train was not an 'all stations' – it did not call at Evercreech New, Masbury, Binegar, Chilcompton, Shoscombe & Single Hill, Wellow or Midford – it was not due at Temple Meads until 7.44pm. Railway enthusiasts would almost certainly have enjoyed spending four hours and more on this journey, but other passengers who simply wanted to get home might have had a rather different view about four hours for an 86½-mile trip. *Photograph: Colin Caddy*

*Left.* The tidy – but not exactly awe-inspiring or imposing – frontage of Bournemouth West station, photographed on 4 September 1965. The station had not seen any S&D trains for more than a month, and as things transpired it was not to see any again. To explain… On 2 August 1965 the line between Branksome and Bournemouth West Junction was 'temporarily' closed while engineering works were carried out in preparation for the electrification of the SR main line. This meant that Bournemouth West station could not be accessed from Branksome, so some S&D trains were diverted to Bournemouth Central and the others started or terminated at Branksome (from where a Hants & Dorset bus service provided a link to Bournemouth West). Some SR trains continued to use Bournemouth West until Sunday 5 September but the following day they, too, were diverted to Bournemouth Central (buses being laid on between there and Bournemouth West). The 'temporary' alternative arrangements for the S&D trains were immediately adopted as permanent so, with the diversion of the remaining SR trains as well, as from Monday 6 September Bournemouth West saw no more passenger trains. However, the station was not 'officially' closed until 4 October 1965. On that same date, the replacement bus services between Bournemouth West and Branksome and Bournemouth Central were withdrawn.
*Photograph: Leslie Freeman;*
*www.transporttreasury.co.uk*

# Bournemouth electrification

## TEMPORARY CLOSURE OF LINES BETWEEN BRANKSOME and BOURNEMOUTH WEST

From Monday August 2nd until Saturday September 4th the lines between Branksome and Bournemouth West Junction will be closed while engineering works are carried out.

Somerset and Dorset Line trains and the 06 43 Weymouth to Bournemouth West train, will in the main, terminate and start from Branksome with a special Hants & Dorset bus service providing a link between Branksome and Bournemouth West stations.

Where the bus service schedule will not allow advertised connections for stations beyond Bournemouth Central to be maintained, the Somerset and Dorset train service will be extended to Bournemouth Central.

Most buses will need to leave Bournemouth West station in advance of the advertised train departure times.

*For train alterations and details of special bus services, see other side.*

British Rail | Southern Region

### Train alterations and Special Bus Service between Branksome and Bournemouth West AUGUST 2nd—SEPTEMBER 4th

**MONDAYS TO FRIDAYS**

| down | TRAIN | departs from Branksome | connecting bus leaves Bournemouth West | connecting bus arrives Branksome |
|---|---|---|---|---|
| 06 57 | Bournemouth West—Broadstone | 07 10 | 06 57 | 07 07 |
| 09 40 | Bournemouth West—Templecombe | 09 44 | 09 31 | 09 41 |
| 11 46 | Bournemouth West—Bristol TM | 11 48 | 11 35 | 11 45 |
| 13 10 | Bournemouth West—Bristol TM | 13 18 | 13 05 | 13 15 |
| 15 40 | Bournemouth West—Bristol TM | 15 44 | 15 31 | 15 41 |
| 17 30 | Bournemouth West—Templecombe | 17 40 | 17 27 | 17 37 |
| 18 48 | Bournemouth West—Bath GP | 18 53 | 18 40 | 18 50 |
| | (starts from Bournemouth Central at 18 46) | | | |

| up | TRAIN | arrives at Branksome | connecting bus leaves Branksome | connecting bus arrives Bournemouth West |
|---|---|---|---|---|
| 06 43 | Weymouth—Bournemouth West | 08 06½ | 08 10 | 08 20 |
| | (diverted to Bournemouth Central due 08 12) | | | |
| 07 35 | Templecombe—Bournemouth West | 09 00 | 09 03 | 09 13 |
| | (diverted to Bournemouth Central due 09 08) | | | |
| 06 00 | Bristol TM—Bournemouth West | 10 46 | 10 49 | 10 59 |
| | (diverted to Bournemouth Central due 10 59) | | | |
| 09 00 | Bristol TM—Bournemouth West | 13 05 | 13 18 | 13 28 |
| 12 30 | Templecombe—Bournemouth West | 13 55 | 18 40 | 14 05 |
| 16 13 | Evercreech Jcn.—Bournemouth West | 18 08 | 18 11 | 18 21 |
| 15 20 | Bristol TM—Bournemouth West | 19 09 | 19 12 | 19 22 |
| 17 55 | Bristol TM—Bournemouth West | 22 19FX / 22 21FO | 22 25 | 22 35 |
| | Notes: FX—Fridays excepted.  FO—Fridays only. | | | |

**SATURDAYS**

| down | TRAIN | departs from Branksome | connecting bus leaves Bournemouth West | connecting bus arrives Branksome |
|---|---|---|---|---|
| 07 10 | Bournemouth West—Bath GP | 07 12 | 06 59 | 07 09 |
| 09 40 | Bournemouth West—Templecombe | 09 44 | 09 31 | 09 41 |
| 11 40 | Bournemouth West—Bristol TM | 11 42 | 11 29 | 11 39 |
| 13 10 | Bournemouth West—Bristol TM | 13 15 | 13 02 | 13 12 |
| 15 40 | Bournemouth West—Bristol TM | 15 44 | 15 31 | 15 41 |
| 18 48 | Bournemouth West—Bath GP | 18 52½ | 18 40 | 18 50 |
| 17 30 | Bournemouth West—Templecombe | 17 34½ | 17 22 | 17 32 |
| 22 05 | Bournemouth West—Templecombe | 22 18 | 22 05 | 22 15 |

| up | TRAIN | arrives at Branksome | connecting bus leaves Branksome | connecting bus arrives Bournemouth West |
|---|---|---|---|---|
| 06 43 | Weymouth—Bournemouth West | 08 00 | 08 03 | 08 13 |
| | (diverted to Bournemouth Central due 08 06) | | | |
| 07 35 | Templecombe—Bournemouth West | 09 00 | 09 03 | 09 13 |
| | (diverted to Bournemouth Central due 09 09) | | | |
| 08 35 | Weymouth—Bournemouth West | 09 46 | 09 53 | 10 03 |
| | (diverted to Bournemouth Central due 09 56) | | | |
| 06 00 | Bristol TM—Bournemouth West | 10 40 | 10 43 | 10 53 |
| | (diverted to Bournemouth Central due 10 50) | | | |
| 09 00 | Bristol TM—Bournemouth West | 13 07 | 13 18 | 13 28 |
| | (diverted to Bournemouth Central due 13 16) | | | |
| 12 30 | Templecombe—Bournemouth West | 13 50½ | 13 55 | 14 05 |
| | (diverted to Bournemouth Central due 13 59) | | | |
| 16 13 | Evercreech Jcn.—Bournemouth West | 18 08 | 18 11 | 18 21 |
| 15 35 | Bristol TM—Bournemouth West | 19 02 | 19 05 | 19 15 |
| 17 55 | Bristol TM—Bournemouth West | 22 22 | 22 25 | 22 35 |

Published by British Railways, Southern Region AD335/A4/23765

*Below.* Bournemouth West was not only the end of the line for S&D trains; prior to the changes of the autumn of 1965 virtually all of the Southern trains which started or terminated in Bournemouth also did so at West station. Usually, the only trains which did *not* use West were those which ran through to and from Weymouth. Consequently, the station saw a wide variety of comings and goings ranging from humble, but splendidly characterful, M7 0-4-4Ts on push-pull duties to Ringwood and Brockenhurst (which is what 30060 is doing here) to the all-Pullman 'Bournemouth Belle' (the stock of which is in the background). This picture was taken on 31 May 1958. *Photograph:www.transporttreasury.co.uk*

# To Glastonbury

*Above*. As explained in one of the earlier photo captions in this book, the Burnham-Wimborne/Poole line was originally the S&D's main line but, when the Evercreech Junction-Bath line opened in 1874, the Evercreech Junction-Burnham section of the original main line was relegated to the status of a branch. The branch became, in a way, the S&D's 'withered arm', and this picture does much to confirm that it led a comparatively quiet existence. Elbow Corner was just under a mile along the branch from Evercreech Junction. The cottage was the accommodation for the crossing keeper, hence its railway-type nameboard. The 'elbow' in question was a more-than-hairpin bend in the road (the lane between Evercreech village and Pylle) immediately to the south of the crossing. By the time this picture was taken on 25 November 1961 the daily passenger service on the branch comprised only five trains each way. Such an infrequent train service was probably just as well, given that these geese were in the habit of waddling across the line. *Photograph: Peter Barnfield*

*Bottom left.* And now we get to Glastonbury & Street station. This spacious establishment was opened to public traffic on 28 August 1854 when the Somerset Central opened its first section of line between Highbridge and Glastonbury. The Somerset Central was originally worked by the Bristol & Exeter Railway, and as the B&E was a broad gauge concern the SCR was necessarily laid with broad gauge rails. The line was extended from Glastonbury to Wells on 16 March 1859, and on 3 February 1862 Glastonbury became a junction when the line was opened from there to Templecombe. By that latter date the Bristol & Exeter's lease on the Somerset Central had expired, so the SCR now worked its own services; conversion from broad to standard gauge soon followed. The station was originally named Glastonbury, the '& Street' suffix not being added until 1886. The neighbouring town of Street had a smaller population than Glastonbury at that time (it was 1901 before Street's population was on a par with that of its neighbour), but it was very important to the railway, principally because the rapidly expanding footwear business of C.& J.Clark was an increasingly good source of revenue. Having mentioned Clarks footwear... yes, the business which Cyrus Clark started at Street in 1825 was the very one which grew and grew and grew to become the Clarks we know today. Cyrus Clark and his brother James had, in fact, been two of the leading lights behind the formation of the Somerset Central Railway. This picture was taken from the east end of Glastonbury & Street station area in 1965. The photographer was standing on the trackbed of the Wells branch which had closed in 1951 – the Wells line and the Evercreech line had run parallel for just over a mile eastwards from the station. The building with the cracked wall on the left is J.Snow & Co's sawmills which had their own private siding. Although the sawmills provided traffic for the railway, the principal goods traffic at Glastonbury & Street was boxes of shoes from Clark's factory at Street. Incidentally, the timber building on the right is still there today, more than forty years after this picture was taken. *Photograph: Peter Barnfield*

*Below.* Glastonbury & Street station might have been one of the most important stations on the S&D in the company's early years, but the public entrance was not very grand. At least, it wasn't by the time this picture was taken in 1964, the overall impression not being helped by the rudimentary canopy supported by scaffolding poles on the outside. By this time the station was served by five trains from Highbridge to Evercreech and six in the opposite direction; if one wanted to travel beyond Highbridge or Evercreech a change of train was required, so most people found that buses were more convenient. Among the options of the period were Bristol Omnibus country service 94 which went from Weston-super-Mare to Street via Glastonbury and service 159 which went from Wells to Bridgwater via Glastonbury. *Photograph: Peter Barnfield*

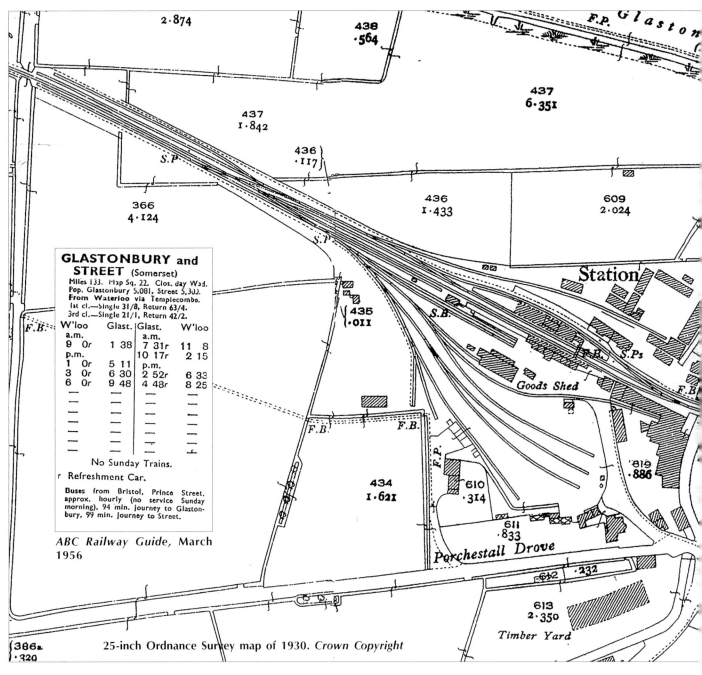

25-inch Ordnance Survey map of 1930. *Crown Copyright*

*Bottom left.* 7F 2-8-0 53807 and 4F 0-6-0 44558 pass slowly through the station with an enthusiasts' special on Sunday 7 June 1964. The signalman is walking towards the train; he is about to exchange single line tokens with the fireman. As can be seen, the train was run by the Home Counties Railway Society. The society had hoped that the second loco would be 53809, but that engine had been condemned the previous month so the 4F had been called upon as a replacement. Nevertheless, it was significant that 53807 and 44558 had actually been built for the S&D, and this special working was the last occasion on which a pair of ex-S&D locos worked together on their 'home' line. The rail tour had started at Waterloo and had run to Bournemouth, where the S&D locos had taken over. A report of the Evercreech-Highbridge leg noted: 'Departure from Evercreech Junction for the branch to Highbridge was at 12.55, five minutes late, but some spirited running on the first section to West Pennard (seventeen minute allowance) saw this completed in just ten minutes and the train was back in front of schedule, which it kept all the way to Highbridge, where the former workshops of the S&D were situated. After running round their train and a lengthy photographic stop, the 4F/7F combination returned along the branch to Evercreech Junction, arriving ten minutes late, where another run round and photographic stop was undertaken. The pair of old veterans then began the assault of the Mendips, but this was not achieved without incident, the train slipping to a stand and having to be restarted, resulting in an eventual arrival in Bath some eighteen minutes late. At Green Park 7023 *Penrice Castle* was waiting to take the train over the Midland line to Gloucester, the first time that one of the class had traversed the branch with a passenger train.' From Gloucester, the tour train returned to London. If memory serves (though don't count on it) the cost of that rail tour was 45/- (£2.25) which, in those days, would have swallowed up around 10-15% of the average weekly wage packet. *Photograph: Hugh Ballantyne*

*Below.* A lovely study of fixtures and fittings and assorted equipment on the main platform at Glastonbury & Street in 1964. The sign above the door of the parcels office warns passengers not to use the barrow crossing. A visitor to the branch in 1952 had noted that 'a sign of the new Western Region regime is clearly evident in that '...the stations at Glastonbury, Evercreech Junction and Cole have been repainted in chocolate and cream, though Glastonbury retains nameboards and notices in Southern Railway green – an odd combination of colours'. As things transpired, Glastonbury kept its green running-in boards until the very end. *Photograph: Peter Barnfield*

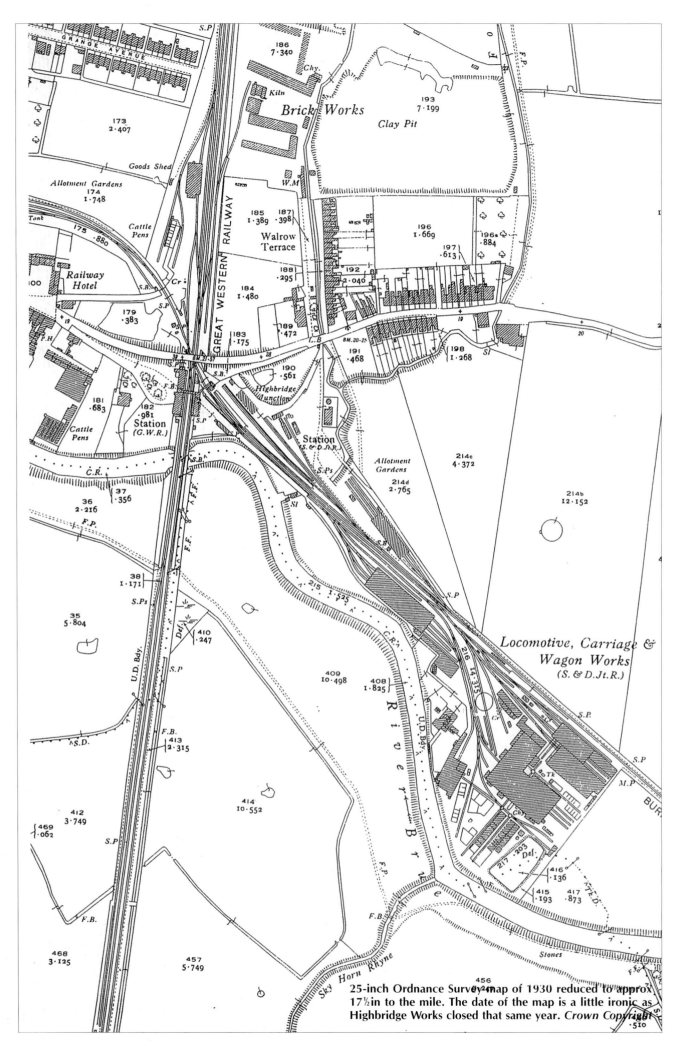

25-inch Ordnance Survey map of 1930 reduced to approx 17½in to the mile. The date of the map is a little ironic as Highbridge Works closed that same year. *Crown Copyright*

# Highbridge

A popular vantage point for observers at Highbridge was the footbridge at the western end of the platforms. Photographer Peter Barnfield took to the footbridge on what had clearly been a showery day in the late summer of 1965. Ivatt 2-6-2T 41216 had arrived with 5.00pm ex-Evercreech Junction (this train was due at Highbridge at 5.55) while another Ivatt waited at Platforms 2 and 3 with one coach and a van which would eventually form the 7.10pm to Evercreech. Highbridge engine shed can be seen in the distance. *Photograph: Peter Barnfield*

From the footbridge in 1965 again… Ivatt 2-6-2T 41216 waits at Platforms 2 and 3 with the 2.20pm to Evercreech Junction. The platform signs confirm that the train *is* standing at two platforms – the line on which it is standing had a platform face on both sides. The platforms at the S&D station and the Western Region station at Highbridge were numbered together but, given that the WR station was on an important main line, it seemed rather eccentric that the S&D platforms came first in the numerical order (platforms 1 to 5) and the WR platforms came last (platforms 6 and 7). Although most of the S&D closed in March 1966 the section between Highbridge and Bason Bridge was retained for milk traffic from the latter. In April 1971 a new connection between the WR line and the S&D was installed almost on the site of the S&D station, but this was not specifically for the milk traffic – it was to handle trains of fly ash from Aberthaw for use in the construction of the M5. This all came to an end on 3 October 1972 when the Highbridge-Bason Bridge section of the old S&D finally closed. *Photograph: Peter Barnfield*

## HIGHBRIDGE.

**Transfer of vehicles between S. & D. and Great Western Railways:—**

(i.) Special arrangements have to be made for the transfer of vehicles from the S. & D. to G.W. Railway and no traffic must be sent via Highbridge without previous advice being given to the District Control Office, Bath.

(ii.) Under no circumstances whatever must Great Western passenger stock, 70 feet or over in length, be transferred over the crossover road leading to and from the G.W. and S. & D. Lines at Highbridge.

(iii.) The signals controlling the operation of transfer between the G.W. and S. & D. Companies must in all cases be worked whether such transfer is made by engine, horse or manual power, and, during darkness, fog or falling snow, a red light must be placed at each end of the vehicles so transferred.

**Special instructions to be observed by all concerned in the transfer of wagons from Great Western to the Somerset & Dorset Line at Highbridge:—**

1.—The Somerset and Dorset goods loop line, which is situated between the " B " and " C " signal boxes, is to be used for the reception of transfer traffic from the Great Western line. The loop is accessible at both ends, and will hold 22 wagons.

2.—The transfer engine will draw the train from the Great Western station direct into the goods loop line through the facing points worked from " B " signal box. The engine will then be detached and let out of the loop through the points worked from " C " box and return at once.

3.—The load of the transfer train must be regulated by the number of wagons that can be accommodated in the loop. When the number of wagons to be transferred exceeds 22, two trips must be made with them, the first being at about 6.30 a.m., and the second at about 7.35 a.m.

4.—In the event of the number of wagons to be transferred exceeding 44, the second train must put off 22 wagons in the goods loop and convey the remainder to, and place them in the Wharf siding, and the S. & D. shunter must be there to assist in the operation.

5.—The guard will be responsible for seeing that the rear of the train is properly protected by the usual tail signal being attached to the rear vehicle, and he must ride in this, or the nearest available vehicle. The shunter must accompany the train for the purpose of detaching the engine and assisting generally.

6.—In the case of a G.W. down goods train arriving at Highbridge with transfer traffic for the S. & D., the wagons, provided they do not exceed 12, may be propelled from the G.W. station to the S. & D. goods loop line. The shunter must accompany the train and satisfy himself that a sufficient number of hand brakes, not less than two, are pinned down on the leading wagons to ensure safe working.

7.—Each train to be signalled on the block telegraph.

*Top left.* Looking westwards into Highbridge station, 20 August 1960. The building on the right accommodated the booking office, the main waiting room and the station master's office. A couple of parcels vans stand in the dock alongside the station buildings and a shiny motor scooter is parked alongside the Gents. *Photograph: Leslie Freeman; www.transporttreasury.co.uk*

*Bottom left.* With five platform faces of its own, Highbridge station was one of the largest on the whole of the S&D. However, size did not equate to grandeur, as evidenced by the waiting room on Platform 5. To be fair, though, since the cessation of 'ordinary' through trains to Burnham in 1951 this platform had been used almost exclusively for arrivals so passengers rarely lingered here. *Photograph: Peter Barnfield*

*Below.* This intriguing view looks westwards from the west end of Platform 5 of Highbridge S&D station in July 1961. We can see the concrete footbridge between the S&D platforms and the WR platforms; the steps on the left give access to/from the S&D arrival platform (Platform 5) and the WR Down platform (Platform 6). A GWR '2251' class 0-6-0 (our crystal ball tells us that it is 3215) is running tender-first along the Burnham branch and is approaching the crossing which took the S&D line over the ex-GWR main line. Part of the canopy of the GWR station can be glimpsed on the far left beyond the footbridge. Note that the first line of this caption refers to the west end of the station, rather than the Up or Down end. We've deliberately avoided using 'Up' and 'Down' for the Highbridge branch as things were not as one might have expected. On most branches around the country 'Down' referred to a trip from the starting point to the end of the line, but on the S&D branch it was Up to Highbridge and Burnham and Down to Evercreech. But this did have a degree of logic. The S&D main line was Up to Bath and Down to Bournemouth, so branch trains travelling from, say, Highbridge to Templecombe were 'Down' all the way. Had the branch been the other way round, our hypothetical branch train would have gone 'Up' on the Highbridge-Evercreech leg but 'Down' on the Evercreech-Templecome leg. Not too many miles from here was an example of how 'Up' and 'Down' could really cause some head-scratching. We refer to the Yatton-Wells-Witham branch: on the Yatton-Wells section it was 'Down' to Wells, while on the Wells-Witham section it was also 'Down' to Wells, thus a train running through from Yatton to Witham started out as a 'Down' train but changed direction, so to speak, at Wells to become an 'Up' train for the rest of its journey. Confused? So are we... *Photograph: Peter Barnfield*

Ex-GWR '2251' class 0-6-0 2204 approaches Highbridge, running tender-first with the empty stock of a Burnham excursion on Saturday 21 July 1962. It is passing Highbridge 'B' signal box and a productive-looking set of allotments and is about to cross the WR main line. It might seem somewhat unusual for an excursion train to contain a parcels van but, as will be explained in one of the other photo captions in this book, this train was an extension of an ordinary scheduled working which would have routinely picked up parcels along the way. To have detached the parcels van for the 'excursion' part of the journey (the Highbridge-Burnham leg) would have been, not only troublesome, but also completely unnecessary. *Photograph: Peter Barnfield*

As mentioned earlier, although the section of line between Highbridge and Burnham-on-Sea lost its scheduled passenger services in October 1951 it continued to accommodate excursion trains until 1962. There were in fact regular excursions on Wednesdays and Saturdays, when the 'ordinary' 1.15pm Evercreech Junction to Highbridge was extended to Burnham. This is what we are looking at here. The date is Saturday 9 September 1961 and the 'extended' 1.15 has just crossed the WR line at Highbridge and is rounding the bend through the town. Don't be deceived into thinking that the train is running 'wrong line'; the line from Highbridge to Burnham was single-track – the lines on the left are sidings, not running lines. The engine at the front is 3F 0-6-0 43682. *Photograph: B.Harding; www.transporttreasury.co.uk*

## *Excursion Bookings*

### EACH WEDNESDAY and SATURDAY
### June 20th to September 8th

ALSO

### *EACH WEEKDAY
### July 30th to August 11th

TO

# BURNHAM-on-SEA

| FROM | DEPART | | | | Return Fares, Second Class |
|------|--------|--|--|--|--------|
| | *Each Wed- nesday | Each Satur- day | Saturdays only, 14th July to 18th Aug. | Daily 30th July to 11th Aug. | |
| | noon | p.m. | a.m. | a.m. | s. d. |
| TEMPLECOMBE .. .. | 12a 0 | 12a 3 | 9a21 | 9a 5 | 8/6 |
| | p.m. | | | | |
| WINCANTON .. .. | 12a 6 | 12a 9 | 9a27 | 9a14 | 7/9 |
| COLE .. .. | 12a14 | 12a17 | 9a35 | 9a22 | 6/9 |
| EVERCREECH JUNCTION .. | 1 15 | 1 20 | 9 55 | 9 55 | 6 3 |
| PYLLE .. .. | 1 20 | 1 25 | 10 0 | 10 0 | 5 9 |
| WEST PENNARD .. | 1 29 | 1 33 | 10 8 | 10 8 | 5 0 |
| GLASTONBURY & STREET ... | 1 40 | 1 45 | 10 20 | 10 20 | 3 6 |
| ASHCOTT .. | 1 48 | 1 53 | 10 28 | 10 28 | 3 0 |
| SHAPWICK .. .. | 1 53 | 1 58 | 10 33 | 10 33 | 2 6 |
| EDINGTON BURTLE .. | 1 59 | 2 4 | 10 39 | 10 39 | 2 3 |
| BASON BRIDGE .. | 2 7 | 2 12 | 10 46 | 10 46 | 1 3 |
| HIGHBRIDGE FOR BURNHAM-ON-SEA .. | 2 12 | 2 17 | 10 51 | 10 51 | 0 9 |
| BURNHAM-ON-SEA arr. | 2 19 | 2 25 | 11 0 | 11 0 | |

**Return from —**
BURNHAM-ON-SEA dep.    6.55 p.m. the same day

*—Also on Mondays to Fridays, 30th July to 10th August.
a—Change at Evercreech Junction.

Children under Three years of age, Free; Three and under Fourteen years of age, Half-fare.
Fractions of a penny reckoned as one penny.

Tickets can be obtained in advance at Booking Stations.

Further Information will be supplied on application to Stations, Agencies, or to Mr. D. S. HART, Divisional Manager, Transport House, Victoria Street, Bristol 1 (Telephone 21001, Extension 641) or Mr. F. P. B. TAYLOR, Commercial Officer, Southern Region, Waterloo Station, London S.E.1

Paddington Station, W.2.
June, 1962.

Printed by J. C. Arrowsmith Ltd., Bristol    (B7, 569)

*Below.* The same train as in our previous picture – the 1.15pm from Evercreech Junction on 9 September 1961 – approaches the level crossing which took the S&D over the A38 at Highbridge. The crossing, its footbridge and the famous landmark of the Lamb Inn can be clearly seen in the mid-distance. Beyond the crossing are the lines leading to Highbridge Wharf (on the left). Going back to the Lamb Inn for a moment… On the wall is the legend Starkeys Ales – our indispensable booklet *Where Have All the Breweries Gone?* tells us that that brewery had been established in Bridgwater in 1887; they originally traded as Starkey Kinght & Co, but on acquiring Thomas Ford & Sons' brewery at Tiverton in 1895 the corporate title was changed to Starkey Knight & Ford. Starkey's and its 400 tied houses were taken over by Whitbread & Co in 1962. *Photograph: B.Harding; www.transporttreasury.co.uk*

_And finally..._

A few of the photographs elsewhere in this book have shown locomotives with their Whitaker tablet apparatus extended. This picture shows the other half of the equation – the lineside tablet catcher. Named after its designer, Alfred Whitaker (the S&D's Locomotive Superintendent from 1889 to 1911), the apparatus was used to exchange the 'tablets' which controlled movements on single-line sections. As we have seen in other pictures, a locomotive – or its tender – was fitted with a short arm which, when out of use, was kept 'tucked in' alongside the engine or tender; when the arm was required for use it was extended at right-angles so that one tablet could be deposited and another collected from the lineside posts. The tablets were contained in pouches – 'neat little Lilliputian mailbags', as they were one described. The lineside posts had a loop on their lower arm – this

was to receive the 'incoming' tablet – and a set of 'jaws' to hold the tablet which had to be collected. The apparatus was very effective and enabled tablets to be exchanged at speeds of up to 60mph. It was later used by the GWR on the Taunton-Barnstaple line and also on Britain's other favourite 'joint' railway – the Midland & Great Northern. All 'main line' engines allocated to the S&D were fitted with catchers. However, 'non resident' engines – ones from other sheds which had been commandeered to help out on summer Saturdays, for example – were not, so the crews needed to remind themselves whether they were on a Whitaker-fitted or a non-fitted engine. (Signalmen also needed advance notice, of course.) Writing in _The Pines Express_ (the excellent journal of the Somerset & Dorset Railway Trust), George Skinner, a passed cleaner at Branksome shed, commented: "The

exchange of the tablet always held the unexpected. One Saturday morning whilst working a train to Bath the engine – being from the North – had no exchanging gear. All went well – we exchanged the pouch by hand with a big steel ring – until we approached Midford. By this time we had a pilot engine in front and the young driver had forgotten that we had no catcher. I reminded the driver that we were approaching the signal box at a fair old speed, and he replied 'we'll take it by hand'. I had been on the line long enough to know not to obey that order, and I told him so. He shouted 'Well, stand aside – I'll do it'. He held on to the footplate handle and put out his arm. I can still hear the whack now. When we got to Bath his arm was black and blue'".
_Photograph: Peter Barnfield_